Insects
and Spiders
of the World

VOLUME 2
BEETLE – CARPET BEETLE

Marshall Cavendish
New York • London • Toronto • Sydney

Marshall Cavendish
99 White Plains Road
Tarrytown, New York 10591

Website: www.marshallcavendish.com

© 2003 Marshall Cavendish Corporation

Library of Congress Cataloging-in-Publication Data
Insects and spiders of the world.
    p.   cm.
    Contents: v. 1. Africanized bee–Bee fly — v. 2. Beetle–
Carpet beetle — v. 3. Carrion beetle–Earwig — v. 4. Endangered
species–Gyspy moth v. 5. Harvester ant–Leaf-cutting ant — v. 6.
Locomotion–Orb-web spider — v. 7. Owlet moth–Scorpion —
v. 8. Scorpion fly–Stinkbug — v. 9. Stone fly–Velvet worm —
v. 10. Wandering spider–Zorapteran — v. 11. Index.
    ISBN 0-7614-7334-3 (set) — ISBN 0-7614-7335-1 (v. 1) — ISBN
0-7614-7336-X (v. 2) — ISBN 0-7614-7337-8 (v. 3) — ISBN 0-7614-7338-6
(v. 4) — ISBN 0-7614-7339-4 (v. 5) — ISBN 0-7614-7340-8 (v. 6) — ISBN
0-7614-7341-6 (v. 7) — ISBN 0-7614-7342-4 (v. 8) — ISBN 0-7614-7343-2
(v. 9) — ISBN 0-7614-7344-0 (v. 10) — ISBN 0-7614-7345-9 (v. 11)
    1. Insects. 2. Spiders.   I. Marshall Cavendish Corporation.

QL463 .I732 2003
595.7—dc21
                                            2001028882

ISBN 0-7614-7334-3 (set)
ISBN 0-7614-7336-X (volume 2)

Printed in Hong Kong

06 05 04 03 02   6 5 4 3 2 1

Brown Partworks Limited
Project Editor: Tom Jackson
Subeditor: Jim Martin
Managing Editor: Bridget Giles
Design: Graham Curd for WDA
Picture Researcher: Helen Simm
Illustrations: Wildlife Art Limited
Graphics: Darren Awuah, Dax Fullbrook, Mark Walker
Indexer: Kay Ollerenshaw

Marshall Cavendish
Editor: Joyce Tavolacci
Editorial Director: Paul Bernabeo

WRITERS
Dr. Robert S. Anderson
Richard Beatty
Dr. Stuart Church
Dr. Douglas C. Currie
Trevor Day
Dr. Arthur V. Evans
Amanda J. Harman
Dr. Rob Houston
Anne K. Jamieson

Becca Law
Professor Steve Marshall
Jamie McDonald
Ben Morgan
Dr. Kieren Pitts
Rebecca Saunders
Dr. Joseph L. Thorley
Dr. Gavin Wilson

COVER: Black widow spider **(Bruce Coleman Collection)**
TITLE PAGE: Black fly **(Bruce Coleman Collection)**

CONTENTS

Beetle	68	Bumblebee	114
Biological control	74	Caddis fly	118
Biting louse	78	Carpenter ant	122
Blackfly	81	Carpet beetle	124
Black widow	84		
Blister beetle	88	*Glossary*	127
Blowfly and bluebottle	90	*Index*	128
Blue butterfly	94		
Bolas spider	96		
Bombardier beetle	97		
Booklouse	100		
Brush-footed butterfly	104		
Bug	106		
Bulldog ant	112		

BEETLE

Scientists think that one out of every four animals on Earth is a beetle. Around 300,000 species are known—far more than any other group of insects. Even so, there may be just as many species still waiting to be discovered.

Over millions of years, the front wings of beetles have evolved into hard covers, called elytra. These meet in a line down the back of the beetle, protecting the hind wings that are used for flying. The rest of the beetle's cuticle (outer covering) is also hard and tough, helping them live in confined spaces without damaging themselves by knocking into hard and sharp objects. Most beetles can fly, but some do so only rarely—to find a mate, for example, or a place to lay their eggs.

Beetles are found on all continents except Antarctica, but they are most common in the tropics. Although the great majority live on land, there are

hind wing

elytra, or wing cases

leg

hardened protective cuticle covers body

▲ *A rhinoceros beetle in flight. The hardened elytra hide the hind wings when the beetle is on the ground. This species gets its name from the hornlike structure on its head.*

◄ *This beetle is a cotton boll weevil. Since people have started growing cotton as a crop, the population of this species has grown enormously.*

also around 5,000 species of water beetles, which have various adaptations to help them breathe under water. Beetles range from tiny species right up to the world's heaviest insect, the goliath beetle of Africa. A giant relative of the June bug, this beetle weighs in at up to 3.5 ounces (100 grams).

A variety of life cycles

The beetle life cycle consists of several distinct stages and, depending on the species, can last for anything from a few weeks to 30 years or more. A beetle egg hatches first into a larva, which looks very different from the adult and whose only activities are eating and growing.

Beetle larvae come in many shapes and sizes. Some (including most water beetle larvae) are carnivorous and long-

ANATOMY OF A WEEVIL

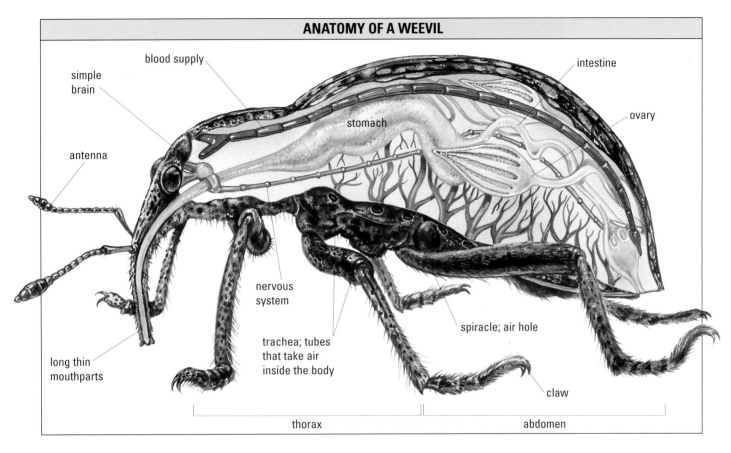

simple brain

blood supply

intestine

antenna

stomach

ovary

nervous system

long thin mouthparts

trachea; tubes that take air inside the body

spiracle; air hole

claw

thorax

abdomen

legged, and they chase or ambush their prey. Many others live inside wood, plant stems, or decaying material; these tend to be soft-bodied and white and may or may not have legs. The larvae of some larger species have been used as food by humans around the world.

The larvae of leaf-eating beetles often look very similar to caterpillars (the larvae of butterflies and moths). The larva molts its skin several times before it is fully grown. In the case of wood- or soil-living species, the larva then generally constructs a protective chamber for itself. After this, it molts to become a pupa (resting stage). The pupa is often white and soft, with the developing legs clearly visible.

The beetle that emerges from the pupa is often long-lived compared with most adult insects; some beetles live for as long as a year or two. The main role of the adult beetle is to find a mate. Beetles often find each other by secreting chemicals called pheromones that attract members of the opposite sex. Sometimes, the sexes

communicate by sound or color. Fireflies are beetles that communicate using flashing lights as signals.

After mating, the female beetle seeks a suitable place to lay eggs. She may be very choosy: some beetles lay eggs only on a single plant species. Generally, the female leaves immediately after the eggs are laid. Some dung beetles and carrion beetles, however, make more elaborate preparations involving both parents. They might carefully bury dung or carrion (dead animals) for their larvae to feed on later. Some beetles feed their newly hatched larvae until they are big enough to fend for themselves.

A variety of lifestyles

Scientists group beetles into more than 130 families. In turn, a single family such as the weevils can contain many thousands of species. Members of the families have become adapted to feed on a huge range of foods. Even so, most beetles have similar kinds of biting mouthparts, both as larvae and adults.

▲ *The internal anatomy of a weevil—a type of beetle—is typical of most beetles.*

KEY FACTS

Name
Rove beetle (Family Staphylinidae)

Distinctive features
Very short elytra that leave most of abdomen exposed

Habitat
Soil, decaying matter, ants' nests

Food
Hunts other insects or feeds on decaying matter

► *This leaf beetle has a remarkable metallic coloration. Many leaf beetles are pests of crop plants.*

thorax

head

antenna

elytra

◄ *This harlequin long-horned beetle gets its name from its coloration and long antennae.*

Wood for food

The larvae of many beetles bore into wood. The majority feed on dead wood or the fungi (plantlike organisms) growing on it. Many species, however, also attack and damage healthy trees. Among families that eat wood are the long-horned beetles, so called because of the long antennae of the adults. This large family attacks both living and dead wood and includes many pest species. The jewel beetle family—named for of its multicolored appearance—has similar habits.

By contrast, stag beetle larvae usually live only in rotting wood. The furniture beetle belongs to another wood-eating family. Bark beetles specialize in tunneling under a tree's bark and often kill the tree, either directly or by spreading diseases such as Dutch elm disease.

Eating plants

There are beetles that eat all parts of a plant—leaves, stems, roots, flowers, and seeds. The two largest leaf-eating families, containing well over 30,000 species each, are the leaf beetles and the weevils. Leaf beetles include pests such as the Colorado potato beetle, as well as the shiny, round-backed tortoise beetles. Weevils, which are often pests, can be recognized by their long snoutlike mouthparts. Their larvae frequently live hidden within stems or flowerheads.

Other types of beetle feed on pollen as adults. Many scientists believe that the first flowers may have been pollinated (had their pollen spread) by beetles, not by bees. Among root-eating larvae are wireworms (the larvae of click beetles) and June bug larvae.

Beetles as predators

Many beetles and their larvae hunt down and eat other small animals. The adults and larvae of ladybugs, for example, both feed on aphids. Other predators include the tiger beetle and related ground beetle families. Dark shiny ground beetles are often seen scuttling away when a stone or log is turned over. Most water beetles are also predatory, as are many of the rove beetles. Rove beetles are a large insect family whose members have very short wing-covers,

The beetles are the best

The beetles are the most successful group of animals on Earth. More than 300,000 species have so far been identified. It is very likely that at least that number of species remain undiscovered. One in three insects are beetles, that is, one in four animals.

There are many reasons for the beetles' incredible success. Their tough protective coating has helped beetles survive in many habitats, both on and under the land, in water, and even inside plants. However, despite their hardy lifestyle, beetles come in thousands of shapes and sizes, with some of the most incredible coloration of any animal.

making them look a little like earwigs. The fireflies, too, are carnivorous, and their larvae feed mainly on snails.

Other food sources

Many beetles live on dead plant material on or below the ground. Others feed on dead animals, or on animal dung. Some beetles are associated with toadstools and other types of fungi, while others live in the nests of termites or ants. Beetles in ants' nests might eat other insects, steal the ants' food, or feed on the ants and their larvae themselves.

▼ *Rove beetles follow a strict routine before they mate. First of all, the male touches the female's rear before joining his sexual organs with hers.*

head

elytra

abdomen

female

male

courting rove beetles

male

sexual organs

thorax

antenna

female

mating rove beetles

71

Defense against enemies

From birds and mammals to tiny parasites, many other creatures view beetles as a potential source of food. In response, beetles have evolved a variety of defense mechanisms. Their tough outer skeleton offers protection against attackers, while both larvae and adults often live hidden within plants or in the soil. Many are active only at night, thus avoiding predation by birds. Beetles do not generally fly from danger, but many can run fast, and others can jump long distances. Weevils often react to disturbances by falling to the ground and playing dead. Some insects have evolved to look like other animals that are poisonous or otherwise dangerous to predators. This is called mimicry. Not many beetles have evolved mimicry, although some that live in ants' nests have come to resemble their hosts.

More active measures include chemical defenses. Ladybugs have poisons in their bodies and advertise this fact with bright warning colors on their wing cases. Many beetles also have glands that produce distasteful or poisonous substances. In the case of bombardier beetles, they can even project these at attackers in the form of a boiling-hot stream of chemicals.

Beetles and humans

Environmental disturbance by humans threatens many beetles, and some, such as the American burying beetle, are now officially protected. Other beetles, however, have benefited from human activities and have become a great nuisance as pests. Crop plants, forestry plantations, building timbers, and stored foods are all regularly attacked by these animals.

Controlling pests

Sometimes, a native beetle becomes a pest. The Colorado potato beetle is one example. The earliest large-scale use of insecticides in the world was directed against this beetle in the mid-19th century. Often, however, a pest is

▶ *An adult tortoise beetle or gold bug (left) and a larva (right) eat their way through a leaf in a woodland in South Africa.*

▼ *A blister beetle mother lays her eggs in a small pit in the ground. She will then cover them in soil to keep them safe from predators.*

brought into a country by accident. The Asian long-horned beetle, for example, is currently causing the death of many North American forest and parkland trees. Because insecticides damage the environment, scientists are looking for alternative ways of controlling these pests. This includes disrupting the mating behavior of the beetles, by releasing huge quantities of their pheromones into the environment, or by introducing a predator or parasite that attacks the beetle.

In some cases, beetles themselves provide the solution to environmental problems, such as the well-known use of ladybugs to attack pests of citrus fruits and other crops. Other beetles are used to control weeds. An unusual problem arose in Australia in the 1920s when cattle dung accumulated on grazing lands. This happened because the native dung beetles were only able to deal with small amounts of kangaroo dung. The problem was solved by importing many thousands of much larger African dung beetles.

SEE ALSO

- *Blister beetle*
- *Bombardier beetle*
- *Carpet beetle*
- *Carrion beetle*
- *Click beetle*
- *Colorado potato beetle*
- *Deathwatch beetle*
- *Dung beetle*
- *Firefly and glowworm*
- *Ground beetle*
- *June bug*
- *Ladybug*
- *Mealworm*
- *Scarab beetle*
- *Soldier beetle*
- *Stag beetle*
- *Tiger beetle*
- *Water beetle*
- *Weevil*

◄ *The goliath beetle is the heaviest insect in the world. This picture shows the insect at half life size.*

BIOLOGICAL CONTROL

Many animals and plants are introduced into new areas by humans, often with disastrous consequences for crops and for native plants and animals. Biological control is one way of reducing the impact of these introductions.

The use of natural enemies to control a particular pest species is termed *biological control*. The natural enemy might be a predator, parasite, or disease that will attack the pest, which may be an insect, a mollusk such as a slug or snail, or a weed. A complete biological control program ranges from choosing a pesticide that will be least harmful to beneficial insects and plants, to releasing one insect to attack another.

Unlike most pesticides, which often kill a wide range of animals, biological control agents are often very specific to a particular pest. Other more beneficial insects, such as honeybees, are not affected by their use. Also, there is no danger of finding pesticide residues in drinking water, food, or the environment as a result of biological control.

However, biological control involves more management and planning than using pesticides, since it requires a greater understanding of the biology of both the pest and its natural enemies. Often, biological control does not give quick, dramatic results, as can be the case when using pesticides.

Natural enemies

Pest species are regularly being introduced into new areas, either accidentally or deliberately. These introduced animals and plants are usually free from the natural predators that kept their numbers in check throughout their natural range, and they sometimes survive and multiply. To deal with these pests, a biological control program often involves importing some of these natural enemies from the pests' country of origin. Large numbers can be bred in laboratories before being released into the wild. Pests are not completely eliminated by biological control; instead,

▲ *Flea beetles are used to control leafy spurge, a weed.*

Combating the spread of water hyacinth

Originally found in central South America, the water hyacinth was introduced to the southern United States during the 1880s. The weed grows extremely fast, and soon waterways were clogged to such a degree that shipping became impossible, and fish and other aquatic life disappeared. Traditional control methods, using machinery to cut away the weed, were unsuccessful.

A biological control program in the 1970s saw the introduction of several species of weevil and the water hyacinth moth. The larvae and adults of these insects feed upon the water hyacinth. This approach has halted the spread of this weed in many areas.

◄ *A parasitic wasp prepares to lay an egg in tunnel dug by the pupa of a corn earworm. After hatching, the larvae will burrow into the pupa and feed on its insides, killing it. Parasitic wasps are often used in biological control, as they usually parasitize one host species.*

their numbers are reduced to levels where crops and animals are unaffected by the presence of the pest species.

U.S. biological control

Over the last 500 years, many pest species have been introduced to North America, and a number of biological control projects have been undertaken. One of the more recent introductions saw the arrival of the blue gum plant louse. Native to Australia, this little insect feeds on eucalyptus plants. It was accidentally introduced to the United States and was discovered in California in 1991. Since then, this louse has spread quickly throughout the coastal area of California and into the Central Valley. It has four or more generations per year, depending on the climate. The adult is gray with orange bands on its abdomen, and it is an active flyer, allowing it to spread far and wide.

The louse deposits clusters of yellow eggs at the base of the leaves and buds of the eucalyptus plant. The young (or nymphs) emerge from the eggs to feed on the plant. The nymphs secrete sticky honeydew, on which a fungus called sooty mold grows. This fungus and the high numbers of lice spoil the appearance of the eucalyptus, which is used in floral arrangements. By feeding on the plant, the lice curb the growth of new shoots and may cause new leaves to become deformed.

Biologists searched for natural enemies of the louse in Australia and New Zealand and found that a parasitic wasp, *Psyllaephagus pilosus*, was an effective natural enemy in these countries. This wasp is mainly black with a hint of metallic green, and at less than one millimeter long, it is tiny. The female wasp lays one egg inside the nymph. The hatching larva feeds on the louse, eventually killing it. Pupation takes place within the remains of the nymph. About three weeks later, a new adult wasp chews its way out.

► *A scientist collects tiny parasitic wasps from the surface of leaves. These wasps will be used to help control whitefly.*

DISTRIBUTION

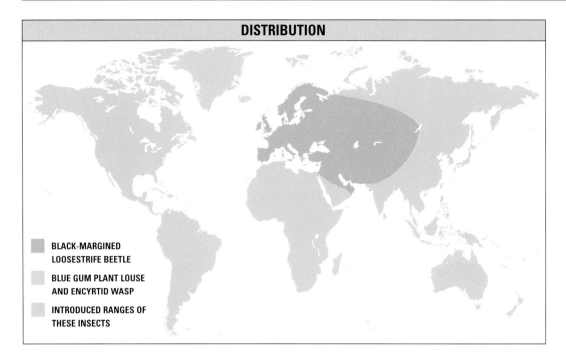

BLACK-MARGINED
LOOSESTRIFE BEETLE

BLUE GUM PLANT LOUSE
AND ENCYRTID WASP

INTRODUCED RANGES OF
THESE INSECTS

Agent
Natural enemy
used in the control
of pest species

**Introduced
species**
Species that do
not occur naturally
in area and have
been brought in by
human activities

Natural enemy
Predator or
parasite

Pest
Feeds on or
outcompetes crops

The wasps were reared in California and released in six different counties. By 1995, the wasp was established at all the release sites, and the numbers of plant lice were greatly reduced. Today, most eucalyptus tree growers have stopped using pesticides and rely on the wasp to control the blue gum plant louse instead. This approach to insect pest management is proving to be highly effective in many cases.

Controlling plants with insects

Another organism that has been introduced into the United States is the purple loosestrife. This plant is native to

▼ *Leaf beetles are sometimes used to control introduced weeds and shrubs. This one is feeding on salt cedar.*

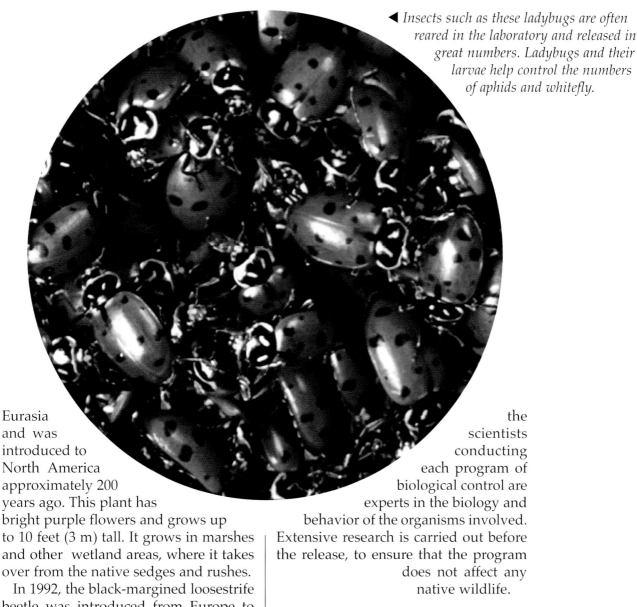

◀ *Insects such as these ladybugs are often reared in the laboratory and released in great numbers. Ladybugs and their larvae help control the numbers of aphids and whitefly.*

Eurasia and was introduced to North America approximately 200 years ago. This plant has bright purple flowers and grows up to 10 feet (3 m) tall. It grows in marshes and other wetland areas, where it takes over from the native sedges and rushes.

In 1992, the black-margined loosestrife beetle was introduced from Europe to North America as part of a biological control program. In spring, the light brown adults emerge and seek out purple loosestrife. Once they have located the weed, they feed on its stems and leaves and lay their eggs in clusters; a single female can lay 300 to 400 eggs each year. The larvae feed on the stems and leaves of the weed. Feeding by the adults and larvae stops the plant from producing flowers and seeds, helping reduce the purple loosestrife population.

The importance of planning

Sometimes, the biological control agents introduced during programs will attack native nonpest species. To prevent this,

the scientists conducting each program of biological control are experts in the biology and behavior of the organisms involved. Extensive research is carried out before the release, to ensure that the program does not affect any native wildlife.

◀ *A cotton bollworm eats a cotton plant. New ways to control this caterpillar using viruses are currently being researched.*

SEE ALSO

- *Aphid*
- *Insecticide*
- *Lacewing*
- *Parasitic wasp*
- *Pest*
- *Scale*

BITING LOUSE

Biting lice are parasites that spend their entire lives on the bodies of their hosts. There are many different types of biting lice, and almost all groups of mammals and birds have their own particular species.

A wide variety of organisms infest the bodies of animals, taking food and shelter from them and giving nothing in return. These organisms are called parasites, and the creatures on which they live are known as hosts. Some parasites (called endoparasites) live inside the bodies of their hosts, while others (called ectoparasites) live on the skin, hair, or fur. Lice are ectoparasites. Some scientists divide lice into two orders, or groups: biting lice (Mallophaga) and sucking lice (Anoplura); other scientists group all lice into

◀ Birds as well as mammals have biting lice. This feather louse lives among the feathers of a duck.

one order, Phthiraptera. Biting lice live on all types of birds, as well as every order of mammals except bats.

Modified to parasitize

All biting lice are small insects, with a body flattened from top to bottom. This shape helps them move easily among fur and feathers and makes it more difficult for their hosts to dislodge them. As their name suggests, they have large jaws for biting through the feathers and fur. Like many parasites that live permanently on their host's body, these lice do not need good eyesight. As a result, their eyes are very small, and are even absent in some species. Similarly, biting lice do not have wings since there is little use for them. Many biting lice have strong hooks on their feet to allow them to hold on to feathers or hair. These claws can be used to distinguish species that live on mammals, which have one claw on each foot, from species that live on birds, which have two claws.

Eggs and nymphs

Biting lice lay their eggs as close to the skin of their host as they can so they are surrounded by as much body heat as possible. The female produces a kind of cement, which she uses to stick her eggs to the hair or feather so the host cannot remove them. The young louse, or nymph, has a novel way of escaping from the egg at hatching time. It sucks air in through a series of tiny holes in the outer casing of the egg and uses it to inflate the eggshell. This causes a circular cap at one end of the egg to blow off, allowing the nymph to crawl out and begin to feed.

Unlike insects such as ants and beetles, biting lice do not undergo complete metamorphosis, the process by which a larval stage changes into a very different-looking adult. Instead, the louse nymph is very similar in appearance to an adult, although it is smaller and paler in color and does not

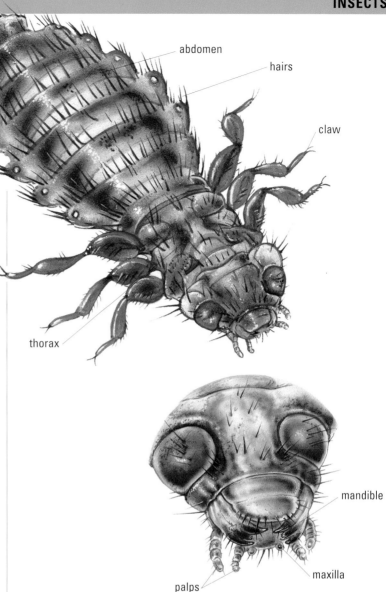

have sexual organs. It sheds its skin three times, each time becoming larger, until it reaches adult size and full sexual maturity. Development from egg to adult takes between three and five weeks, and the louse lives for only a few months. Most lice spend their entire life on a single host animal, only moving to another host when close contact occurs, allowing the lice to crawl from one host to the other.

Digesting fur and feathers

Most species of biting lice feed on skin debris, or even eat the fur or feathers of their host. Many of these lice have bacteria in their gut that help them digest the tough protein, called keratin,

▲ *Modified for success: biting lice have flattened bodies, with claws on each leg. They have strong mouthparts that can bite through fur or feathers. The louse uses its mandibles and maxillae like jaws, to chop up and hold its food. The sensitive palps taste and manipulate the food.*

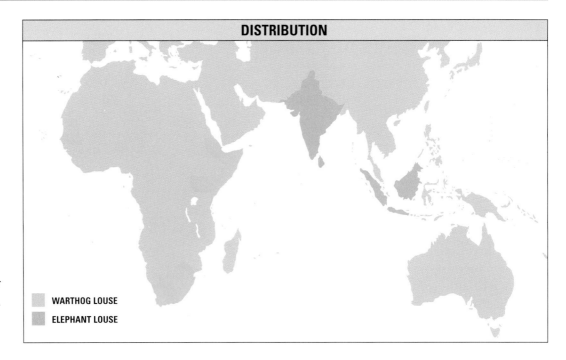

DISTRIBUTION

WARTHOG LOUSE
ELEPHANT LOUSE

▼ *A hog louse under high magnification. The large claws at the ends of each limb are essential for clinging on to the host.*

SEE ALSO

- *Anatomy and physiology*
- *Booklouse*
- *Flea*
- *Larva, nymph, and pupa*
- *Parasitic fly*
- *Sucking louse*

of which fur and feathers are made. Other species have proteins called enzymes in the gut that do the same job. Some biting lice may accidentally draw blood when chewing at the base of fur or feathers and will eat it. However, unlike sucking lice, their close cousins, biting lice do not generally live on the blood of their hosts. The only exceptions to this are the elephant louse and the warthog louse. These lice have especially strong mouthparts, which they use to pierce through the tough hide of their hosts.

Lice, flies, and bats

Every group of warm-blooded animals has a range of associated lice, except one—bats. In bats, the role of the biting lice has been taken by two very specialized groups of flies. The presence of these flies prevented any bat-specific species of lice from being able to evolve. Although they are only very distantly related, these flies look quite like lice, with similar adaptations such as a flattened body, absence of wings, and claws at the end of each leg. The process whereby unrelated animals with similar lifestyles develop similar adaptations is called convergent evolution.

Well-traveled insects

There are around 2,900 species of biting lice known to science, many of which can live only on a single bird or mammal species. However, there are many more waiting to be discovered. Some species are now found around the globe, since they have traveled with their hosts overseas to new continents as part of human trading activities.

BLACKFLY

Most people find blackflies annoying for their itchy bites. However, these insects have affected the lives of millions of people around the world by giving them a terrible, blinding disease.

Many species of birds and mammals unwittingly provide a meal for bloodsucking blackflies. There are around 1,750 known species of blackflies worldwide, including 255 species in North America. The waterborne larval stages are important food sources for a range of aquatic invertebrate predators, fish, and waterfowl.

Growth and development

Like other types of flies, there are four stages in a blackfly's life cycle: egg, larva, pupa, and adult. The first three stages live in moving fresh water. The larva is a sausage-shaped creature that bears a pair of rakelike appendages (called labral fans) on the top of its head. It attaches to rocks using a circle of hooks on the abdomen, while the fans filter out plantlike algae, bacteria, and other food from the water current. The fans are then folded into the mouth.

Larvae pass through about seven molts. Mature larvae spin a silken cocoon that varies in form from a shapeless sac to an elaborate boot-shaped structure. After finishing the cocoon, the larva retreats inside and transforms into a pupa. A pair of branched, feathery gills that project forward from the pupa allow it to breathe. Once fully developed, the adult emerges through a slit in the cocoon and rises to the surface in a bubble of gas.

Adult blackflies

Adults are 0.06 to 0.25 inches (1.5 to 6.3 mm) long and generally gray to black. They are stocky, humpbacked

flies with cigar-shaped antennae and dark veins along the front edge of the wings. Males are easily distinguished from females by the presence of enormous eyes that join together at the tops of their heads.

In most blackfly species, males assemble in swarms. The swarms congregate near a prominent object called a swarm marker. This can be a large stone or tree stump, or below an overhanging branch. Females flying into such swarms are quickly mated. Male blackflies are generally short-lived, but females may survive for up to a month. Both sexes feed on sugary food such as nectar and aphid honeydew. However, to develop their eggs, the females of some species require a blood meal.

▲ *A newly emerged adult blackfly rests on a water plant before taking flight. Below the surface on the left, a pupa can be seen attached to the underside of another frond.*

KEY FACTS

Name
Simulium venustum
(no common name)

Distinctive features
Dark-bodied; biting mouthparts; brilliant white bands on legs

Habitat
Clean streams throughout much of North America

Behavior
Female bites mainly at dusk but also at dawn

Breeding
Eggs are laid on stream vegetation

Food
Larva feeds on microscopic organic particles such as algae and bacteria; adult female feeds on mammalian blood

Lifespan
Female lives for a month

Size
Adult: 0.14 inches (3.5 mm) long

DISTRIBUTION

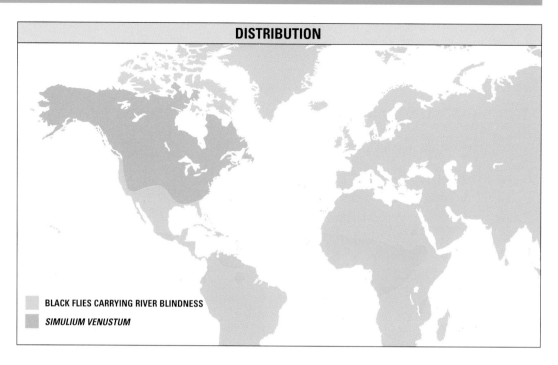

☐ BLACK FLIES CARRYING RIVER BLINDNESS

■ *SIMULIUM VENUSTUM*

Bloodsuckers

Bloodsucking females find their hosts using a combination of cues. At long range, the flies may detect the carbon dioxide that the bird or mammal breathes out. Closer in, they use the heat and odor of the host to guide them. They use their bladelike mouthparts to pierce the skin and inject an anticoagulant into the wound. The anticoagulant stops the blood from clotting, allowing it to flow freely. It takes between three and six minutes for the female to eat her fill. The bite causes an itchy bump that may last for two weeks. Sometimes, bites cause an allergic reaction, resulting in an illness called blackfly fever.

Medical importance

As well as being irritating, the female blackfly can also transmit disease-causing organisms into an animal when

▶ *A female blackfly sucks blood through the skin of a human hand. Her body swells up as she takes in the food.*

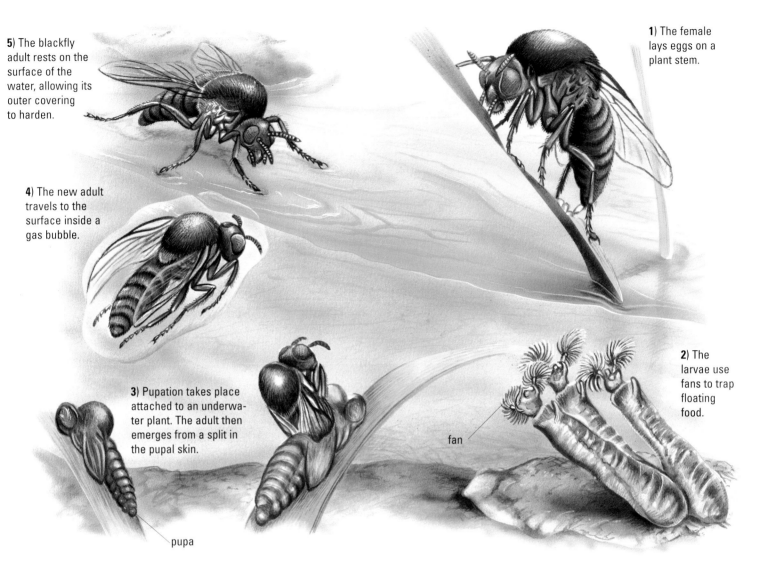

5) The blackfly adult rests on the surface of the water, allowing its outer covering to harden.

1) The female lays eggs on a plant stem.

4) The new adult travels to the surface inside a gas bubble.

3) Pupation takes place attached to an underwater plant. The adult then emerges from a split in the pupal skin.

fan

2) The larvae use fans to trap floating food.

pupa

she bites. Many of the species that feed on birds transmit a malaria-like disease to wild and domestic fowl, often resulting in death. Some of the species from the United States and Canada are known to transmit parasitic worms to moose, deer, and bears.

The most serious disease transmitted by blackflies is river blindness. This disease affects people throughout tropical Africa and Central America. Tiny parasitic roundworms enter the host through the wound made by a feeding blackfly. The worms multiply and cause a variety of symptoms, including severe itching and large swellings under the skin. Dead worms may build up in the eyes, causing blindness. When another blackfly bites, it takes in some of

the worms with the blood; these worms live in the flight muscles of the fly, increasing in number, before entering another human host. At least 17 million people are infected with river blindness.

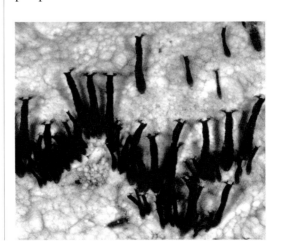

▲ *Blackflies spend their larval stages under water.*

◄ *Blackfly larvae are filter-feeders. They hang in the current sieving their food.*

SEE ALSO
- *Fly*
- *Disease carrier*
- *Gnat*
- *Mosquito*
- *Sand fly*

83

BLACK WIDOW

As one of the most venomous spiders in the world, the black widow is both admired and feared by people. However, these deadly hunters are more likely to kill each other than a human.

Black widows are the most famous spiders in the family called comb-footed spiders. These spiders build irregular shaped webs called cobwebs with lines of sticky silk that reach to the ground. Prey are caught by the sticky silk, and the vibrations caused by the struggles of the trapped animal alert the spider, who then moves in for the kill.

Using tiny combs on the feet of their last pair of legs, comb-footed spiders pay out sheets of sticky silk from their spinnerets to quickly wrap up their prey before delivering a fatal bite. Comb-footed spiders build their cobwebs close to a crevice or other suitable hiding place. They spend most of their time waiting for prey on the edge of their webs near the crevice.

Where are black widows found?
There are three species of black widows in the United States. The western black widow lives throughout western North America, while the northern black widow is found in the east and into

▶ *A female black widow spins silk around a struggling scorpion caught in the spider's web.*

▼ *This female western black widow shares its web with a much smaller male.*

Name
Southern black widow (*Latrodectus mactans*)

Distinctive features
Female: black with large, round abdomen with red hourglass pattern underneath; male: smaller and tan-colored

Habitat
Found from sea level to 8,000 feet (2,400 m) in sheltered areas such as burrows, under stones, and in houses

Behavior
Traps prey in irregular webs

Breeding
Males court females in their webs and are sometimes eaten

Food
Insects and other arthropods

Lifespan
Matures in three months; males live for a few weeks; females live from one to three years

Size
Female body: 0.6 inches (1.5 cm); legspan: 1.5 inches (4 cm); male body: 0.25 inches (6 mm); legspan: 1 inch (2.5 cm)

Canada. The southern black widow is more widespread and lives in much of eastern and southern United States, Mexico, Central and South America, and the Caribbean. Two additional species of widow spiders occur in Florida. The red widow lives only in the sand pine scrub habitat found in that region, while the brown widow is found throughout the tropical areas of the world, especially mainland Africa.

Vital statistics

The female black widow may reach one and a half inches (38 mm) long with the legs extended. All female black widows are glossy black with a large rounded abdomen. They have red or white markings down the upper side of their abdomen. A distinctive red hourglass marking on the underside of the abdomen of both sexes is easily visible on the female as she hangs upside down in the web.

The adult male is much smaller than the female, at around one inch (26 mm) long with the legs extended. The males' tan or black bodies are much flatter and are marked with white streaks on the top of the abdomen. Because of their

DISTRIBUTION

■ SOUTHERN BLACK WIDOW
■ NORTHERN BLACK WIDOW
■ WESTERN BLACK WIDOW

female

pedipalp

male

▲ *A male black widow plucks at the web of the much larger female as he begins the mating ritual. Scientists think this plucking behavior tells the female that the spider is a mate, rather than a meal.*

small size and short fangs, male black widows often go unnoticed and are completely harmless to humans.

Mating—a risky business

Upon maturity, the male spins a small web into which he deposits a droplet of sperm. He draws up the fluid with organs on the tips of his pedipalps (leglike structures at the sides of the mouth). He then wanders off in search of the female's web. By tugging on the web, the male lets her know that he is a mate and not a meal. Meanwhile, he vibrates his abdomen on the web. If receptive, the female will respond with similar movements. He cautiously approaches her, stroking her legs with his. If she remains receptive, he will spin a delicate web around her before placing the sperm in her body. The male

exits her web carefully, to avoid being mistaken for prey. Very occasionally, the male is not fast enough when leaving the web, and he is captured and eaten by his mate. It is this behavior of the female that has earned the name "black widow."

The female black widow deposits 300 to 500 round eggs in a silken egg sac that looks and feels like parchment. The sac

Spider bite

The venom of the black widow is very powerful. It affects the human nervous system, causing tenderness at the site of the bite, severe muscular pain and stiffness, sweating, high blood pressure, and vomiting; it also increases the heart rate. However, black widows are not aggressive spiders. They usually try to escape and will only bite if they are pressed against the body. If bitten by a black widow, put a bag of ice on the wound, keep the patient calm, and seek medical treatment immediately. Doctors use an antivenin to stop the poison's effects.

protects the eggs from predators and parasites. After two to four weeks, the eggs hatch, although the spiderlings remain in the sac until they have molted. Then they use their saliva to dissolve the silk and escape. Like the males, the small fangs of spiderlings make them harmless to humans.

The young spiderlings are usually orange and white and may take up to four months to mature. In warmer climates, they mature faster. The male molts an average of five times before reaching maturity, while the female usually molts seven to nine times. Female black widows often live for a year or two, and even longer in captivity, while the adult males live for only a few weeks, even if they do survive the jaws of a mated female.

Venomous predators

Black widow spiders are well known for their venomous bite. Ounce for ounce, the venom of black widows is 15 times more potent than that of a rattlesnake. However, the amount of venom injected into the wound is relatively small. Because of this, very few people die from black widow bites, although it is still extremely important that people who have been bitten receive medical attention as soon as possible.

Black widows only bite humans when they cannot escape. They prefer to stay out of the way, spinning their webs in stumps, under rocks and stones, in abandoned rodent burrows, and occasionally in the closets, attics, and basements of people's homes.

Silken strength

A black widow's web is made of extremely strong silk, with each strand having ten times the strength of a steel wire of the same thickness. In the past, the silk produced by female widows was harvested and used as cross hairs in gun sights.

Black widows will eat any animal that becomes entangled in their web, including insects, other spiders, and even

small vertebrates such as lizards and mice. The black widow immobilizes prey by tightly wrapping it in a blanket of silk. Then the spider sinks its fangs into the prey to kill it and liquefy its internal organs. The resulting half-digested mush is then sucked out and eaten by the spider.

Black widow numbers are kept in check by several predators and parasites. Alligator lizards prey upon black widows. The blue mud-dauber wasp provides its young with chewed-up black widows. The larvae of several parasitic flies and wasps devour the black widow's eggs inside the egg sac before they hatch. Black widows also fall prey to other comb-footed spiders.

SEE ALSO
- *Bolas spider*
- *Crab spider*
- *House spider*
- *Jumping spider*
- *Ogre-faced spider*
- *Orb-web spider*
- *Spider*
- *Spitting spider*
- *Wolf spider*

▼ *The female black widow has a red hourglass pattern on the underside of her abdomen.*

BLISTER BEETLE

These beetles have a remarkable life cycle and spend much of the larval stage in the nests of bees. There, they live off their hosts, stealing food and feeding on bees' eggs and grubs.

KEY FACTS

Name
Meloe franciscanus (no common name)

Distinctive features
Black, sometimes slightly shining; short wing covers expose swollen abdomen

Habitat
Deserts of southwestern United States

Behavior
Adults secrete irritating chemical

Breeding
Lays up to 3,000 eggs; larvae group together to mimic female bee and hitch ride on male bee; larvae then pass from male to female during mating and are carried back to nest by female bee

Food
Adults feed on plants; larvae feed on pollen, nectar, eggs and young in bees' nest

Lifespan
Becomes adult four months after hatching; adults live for up to three months

Size
Length: 0.3 to 0.5 inches (9 to 13 mm)

although a few unusual species are also known to feed on the egg cases of grasshoppers. Adults of the bee parasites lay their eggs on plants. After hatching, the small, flattened, very active larva (called a triungulin) climbs up the plant and onto the flowers, where it awaits the arrival of a bee. It then uses its speed

◀ *An adult blister beetle on a flower. These insects can secrete irritating chemicals from their leg joints if threatened. Doctors are studying this chemical to see if it can treat infections.*

Blister, or oil, beetles are medium to large black or brown beetles. They are often marked with red, yellow, or white spots, and some have a metallic shine. They are most frequently found in hot, arid areas. There are about 2,500 species known worldwide, with more than 300 species in North America. Adult blister beetles are plant feeders often seen in large numbers on their food plants during the daytime. When abundant, some species can sometimes become serious crop pests.

Parasitizing bees

Adults of some flower-feeding species have developed elongated mouthparts that look like those of adult butterflies and which are used for nectar feeding. The larvae of most blister beetles are parasitic in the nests of wild bees,

DISTRIBUTION

MELOE FRANCISCANUS

◀ *A spotted blister beetle on a flower. The adults of this species often feed on potato leaves.*

SEE ALSO

- *Beetle*
- *Bumblebee*
- *Defense*
- *Honeybee*
- *Metamorphosis*
- *Mimicry*

and agility to attach itself to the bee, which flies back to the nest carrying the parasite along. This process, where one insect carries another, is called phoresy. Once in the nest, the triungulin molts and becomes a much less active, grublike larva. This form eats nectar, pollen, and the occasional bee's egg or larva. After pupation, the adult beetles generally move away. There are, however, some species that have non-flying adults, which continue to live inside the bee nest.

Bee-duping beetles

Recently, it has been discovered that rather than climbing onto flowers to wait for a bee, the triungulin larvae of *Meloe franciscanus* have developed a tactic to attract a bee to them.

A group of the larvae clump together on a plant, usually the tip of a twig, and take on the size and shape of an adult female bee. They also release chemical attractants into the air, and when a male bee lands to investigate, the larvae immediately attach themselves to its body. Having been duped, the bee flies off with a burden of beetle larvae. When

the male bee mates with a real female, the beetle larvae switch over to the female bee. The female then carries the larvae back to the nest.

The body fluids of all blister beetles contain an irritating chemical called cantharidin. The beetles secrete this chemical (usually at the joints of the legs) to ward off predators. Cantharidin causes blistering when it comes into contact with human skin, hence the common name blister beetle.

▼ *Some blister beetle larvae clump together to mimic the shape of a female bee. When a male bee attempts to mate with the fake female, the larvae climb onto the male and are carried off.*

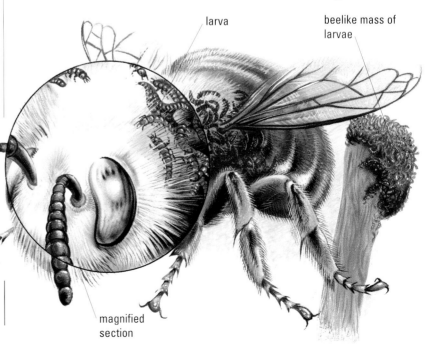

larva

beelike mass of larvae

magnified section

BLOWFLY AND BLUEBOTTLE

These flies feed on a variety of dead, decaying, and sometimes living material. Some are economically damaging to farmers; others are an important tool in police investigations.

Among the most familiar and common of all insects, blowflies can often be seen buzzing noisily around homes looking for food. There are about 1,000 species of blowflies worldwide. Most are metallic blue or green and have bodies covered in stout black bristles. Adult blowflies have only one pair of wings; their hind wings are reduced to form drumstick-shaped structures called halteres. Halteres provide the blowfly with balance information as the insect flies around.

Blowflies have a very good sense of smell due to the feathery tips of their antennae, called arista, which can detect the odors of food from long distances away. The majority of adult blowflies use their complex mouthparts for sucking up liquid food. Blowflies usually feed on sweet food, such as rotting fruit or nectar from flowers. Female blowflies need protein to produce their eggs. They get this by feeding on dead animals or dung.

Blowfly larvae

The larvae of blowflies are often called maggots. They are carrot-shaped, pale, and do not have legs. Maggots move by sending ripples along the length of their soft bodies. In most species, the head of the maggot (the pointed end) contains only the mouthparts. The rear end of the maggot has two dark spots that are often mistaken for eyes. These spots are spiracles, small pores through which the maggot breathes. By having these breathing holes at the rear end, maggots can breathe while burrowing into their

▲ *Although adult* Lucilia *blowflies feed on nectar, the maggots of some species feed on the flesh of live animals, causing considerable economic damage.*

DISTRIBUTION

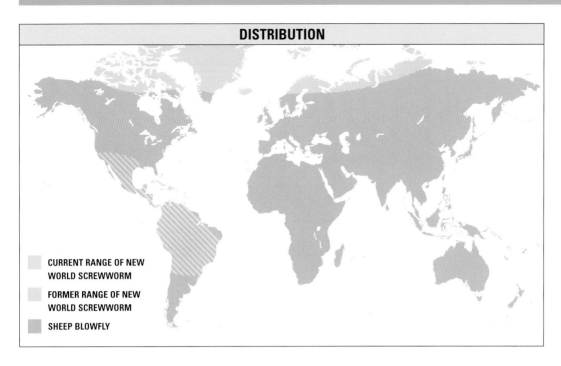

CURRENT RANGE OF NEW WORLD SCREWWORM

FORMER RANGE OF NEW WORLD SCREWWORM

SHEEP BLOWFLY

KEY FACTS

Name
Sheep blowfly
(*Lucilia sericata*)

Distinctive Features
Metallic green;
red eyes

Food
Adults eat dead
matter; larvae feed
on sheep flesh

Breeding
Eggs laid on
sheep; pupate in
cracks in ground

food. The maggots grow through a number of stages. When fully grown, they are around 0.4 inches (1 cm) long. The larvae of most blowflies feed on decaying organic matter, such as dead animals. The maggots of some species of blowflies feed on live animals, and a few are parasites of earthworms.

Maggots feed for two to ten days and then wriggle away from their food. Their skin hardens, forming a dark, barrel-shaped structure called a puparium. The puparium protects the maggot as it changes into an adult fly. Inside the puparium, the maggot changes into a pupa, and its body liquefies before re-forming as an adult fly.

The new fly emerges from the puparium by inflating a sac on the front of its head. This splits the end of the puparium open, allowing the fly to wriggle out. The skin of the fly hardens, the wings expand, and the adult blowfly is then ready to feed and mate.

Flesh eaters

Some of the most important species of blowfly are those with maggots that sometimes feed on the flesh of live animals. These include the sheep blowflies *Lucilia sericata* and *Lucilia cuprina*. Both flies are roughly 0.4 inches

(1 cm) long and are metallic green. These blowflies live all around the world. This is because they have been accidentally carried to other places by sheep or people over the last few hundred years. Female sheep blowflies are attracted to sheep and are not usually found indoors. They lay around 200 eggs on a damp fleece. The eggs

▼ *Maggots on a dead animal. The spots on these larvae are not eyes but spiracles through which the maggots breathe while burrowing into their food.*

▲ *A bluebottle feeding on meat. The fly uses saliva to partially digest the food before sucking up the resulting soup.*

hatch, and the maggots feed on the flesh of the sheep; this is known to farmers as sheep strike or blowfly strike. After feeding, the maggots fall from the sheep and form puparia. The life cycle of these insects takes around four to six weeks. Adult flies live for roughly seven days in the wild. Sheep strike can kill if left untreated; as many as three million sheep may be killed by blowfly activity every year in Australia. Farmers dip their sheep in chemicals to kill the blowfly larvae. If used excessively and without care, these chemicals can be harmful to the environment and to the health of the farmers. Biologists are investigating other ways of combating blowfly strike.

Another important blowfly is the New World screwworm. This fly is around 0.5 inches (1.3 cm) long, and it is shiny bluish green. It lives in Mexico, Central America, the Caribbean, northern Chile, Argentina, and Uruguay. Females live

for seven to ten days and can lay between 200 and 500 eggs every two or three days. They lay eggs near the nostrils, eyes, mouth, and ears of almost all warm-blooded livestock, wildlife, and humans. The eggs hatch, and the maggots burrow into the flesh, where they feed for a week or so before dropping to the ground and forming puparia. The entire life cycle can be completed in 24 days but takes longer if the weather is cold. A program to lower

Healing wounds

Many diseases are caused by insects, but due to scientific research some are now being cured by insects, too. Doctors have discovered that the feces of certain blowflies contain a substance that helps wounds to heal more quickly. Amazingly, the wounds also benefit from being filled with maggots. These fly larvae produce natural antibiotics, chemicals that kill bacteria, which can cause infections in cuts.

screwworm numbers in Texas was started in 1957, since these flies attacked hundreds of thousands of animals throughout the state each year, costing millions of dollars. Large numbers of sterilized male flies were released to mate with females. Since screwworm flies only mate once, this dramatically reduced the numbers of young. The technique was highly successful, and the New World screwworm has been eradicated from the United States. Similar methods are now being used in other parts of the fly's range.

Helpful flies

Blowflies are generally considered a nuisance, since we often find some species in our homes. For example, the bluebottle is sometimes attracted indoors by the smell of fresh meat or fish. It then buzzes loudly around the room and against the window until it finds a way out or is swatted. The bluebottle is a blue-gray fly, 0.5 inches (1.2 cm) long, with dark red eyes. They feed on edible garbage of all kinds, as well as fresher food left unattended before being cooked. Although many people do not like blowflies, and some spread disease, they are a very important part of the natural environment. Without fly maggots feeding on decaying flesh, dead animals would take much longer to rot.

Blowflies can be useful to humans. For example, different species of blowfly prefer to lay their eggs on dead animals at different times after the animal has died. When the dead body of a person is found, police experts can estimate the time of death by identifying the blowfly maggots present and by considering the stage of their development, the temperature, and other environmental conditions. In this way, blowflies can provide valuable information about crime. The use of insects to provide such data is called forensic entomology.

Blowfly maggots are sometimes used by doctors to clean wounds. The maggots eat away at dead tissue and their saliva contains antibiotics, which prevent the wound becoming infected.

◀ *Blowflies eat a range of organic matter. These are feeding on fungi.*

SEE ALSO

- *Entomology*
- *Fly*
- *Housefly*
- *Insecticide*
- *Pest*
- *Warble fly and botfly*

BLUE BUTTERFLY

The blue butterflies comprise a diverse family, which also includes the copper and hairstreak butterflies. Many have very strange life cycles, and some have close relationships with ants.

◄ A red-banded hairstreak butterfly sits on a stalk of wheat. Despite its color, this species belongs to the blue butterfly family.

wingspan of only 0.3 inches (8 mm). Scientists often divide the family into several different groups, including the blues, coppers, and hairstreaks.

Adults, eggs, and caterpillars

Adult blue butterflies feed on nectar from flowers and the sugary excretions of aphids. Many of the smallest species are weak fliers and spend their entire lives in a small area. The males are often brighter

▼ A common blue butterfly feeding on fleabane. The undersides of the wings are green, helping the butterfly to remain inconspicuous at rest.

Most members of the blue butterfly family are small and brightly colored. Despite their name, however, they are not necessarily blue. Although many do have a striking iridescent blue or violet color, others are red, orange, copper-colored, or green. Often, it is only the upper sides of the wings that are colored, while the undersides are drab. This helps to provide camouflage when the wings are closed.

Around one quarter of all butterflies are blues; the family contains about 4,000 species, including the world's smallest butterfly, *Micropsyche ariana*, from Afghanistan, which has a

DISTRIBUTION

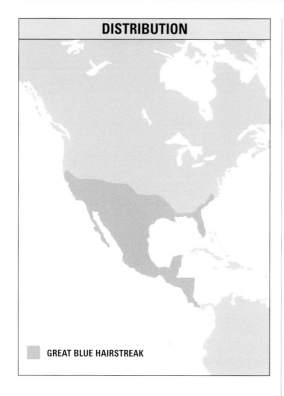

GREAT BLUE HAIRSTREAK

Name
Great blue
hairstreak (*Atlides
halesus*)

**Distinctive
Features**
Iridescent blue-
purple wings, tails
on hind wings

Breeding
Lays eggs on
mistletoe in trees

Food
Caterpillar:
mistletoe leaves;
adult: nectar

- *Brush-footed
  butterfly*
- *Glasswing
  butterfly*
- *Moth and
  butterfly*

---

caterpillars have molted several times and grown, ants pick them up and haul them back to their nests to milk their nutritious secretions. In return, the ants let the caterpillars eat their larvae.

The caterpillars develop into chrysalises within the ants' nest and stay there until spring, when they emerge as adults. The large blue's dependence on wild thyme and a particular ant species has made it unable to cope with changes to its habitat brought about by humans. As a result, the species became extinct in England in 1979, although it has been reintroduced. A similar fate awaits other blue butterflies with unusual life cycles.

Tropical diversity

Blue butterflies are at their most diverse in the tropics, where the most brilliantly colored species are found. Many blues have thin streamers on their hind wings, with spots nearby. These spots resemble eyes, and the streamers imitate antennae—this false head dupes predators into attacking the rear end of the butterfly, rather than the more vulnerable front end. This increases the butterfly's chances of escape. Tropical hairstreaks often live in the rain forest canopy. Their pupae attach to leaves in the treetops and are sometimes camouflaged as bird droppings to fool predators.

---

than the females, and sometimes look so different they appear to be separate species. After mating, most blue butterflies lay small, bun-shaped eggs on vegetation, particularly on plants that are rich in protein, such as members of the pea family.

The caterpillars that hatch out are very distinctive. They are green or brown and almost like pillbugs in shape, with short, squat bodies and arched backs. Their small heads sometimes appear to be buried in the thorax (midbody). The caterpillars feed on leaves, flowers, buds, and seed pods, and some species also eat small insects such as aphids.

Blue butterflies and ants

Many blue butterfly caterpillars have a special relationship with ants. The caterpillars secrete a nutritious fluid from glands on their abdomen, and this is eagerly lapped up by ants. In return, the ants protect the caterpillars from predators, such as spiders. Caterpillars of the European large blue butterfly have taken this relationship a step further. Female large blues lay their eggs on thyme plants, on which the caterpillars feed when they are young. When the

▶ *The
turquoise
hairstreak has
eyelike spots
and antennae-
mimicking
streamers on its
hind wings.*

eyespot

streamer

BOLAS SPIDER

No other spider lassoos its prey like the bolas spider.

Most orb-web spiders use a web to catch their prey—they wait for prey to blunder on to the sticky threads. However, the bolas spiders, which make up about 50 species in this group, use a very different method.

Lassooing prey

Bolas spiders are extremely specialized hunters, and they are experts at imitating the smells of other animals. As spiderlings, they emit chemicals that are very similar to the pheromones released into the air by certain female flies. Pheromones are smelly chemicals that are released by animals. The smell draws in male flies, which the spiderlings grab with their legs and eat. After becoming adults, the males continue to hunt like this, but the females grow larger and hunt in another way.

At nightfall, the female hangs upside down from a twig and spins a single line of silk, with a sticky ball at the end—this is called the bolas. A blend of chemicals emitted into the air mimics the pheromones released by female moths, luring male moths in to investigate. Some bolas spiders swing their sticky trap continuously, while others are more selective: they wait until the moth is near before launching the bolas.

When the spider lands a direct hit, the bolas penetrates the scaly covering of the moth and sticks to the skin, allowing the spider to draw in the moth. If the spider has not captured a moth within half an hour or so, it eats the silk and starts again, since the ball loses its stickiness with time.

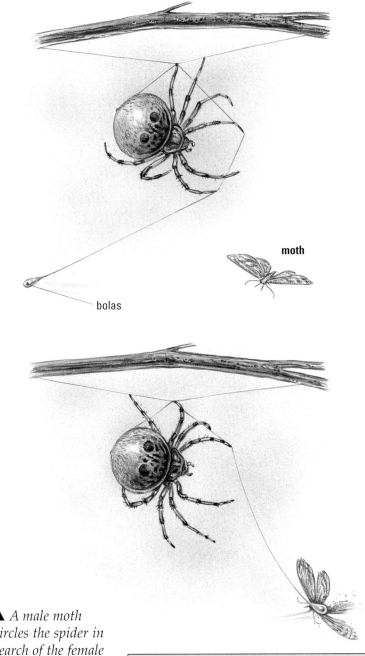

moth

bolas

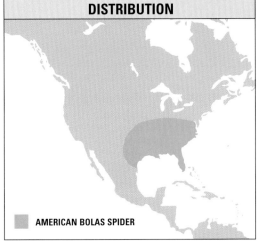

▲ *A male moth circles the spider in search of the female moth he believes is there. The spider swings her bolas until it hits the moth. A female bolas spider usually catches about two moths every night.*

SEE ALSO
- *Mimicry*
- *Orb-web spider*
- *Spider*

DISTRIBUTION

AMERICAN BOLAS SPIDER

BOMBARDIER BEETLE

These beetles have one of the most remarkable and powerful chemical defense systems in the animal kingdom: they are able to squirt a hot cocktail of poisons at potential predators.

There are hundreds of species of bombardier beetles found throughout the world. They belong to the ground beetle family, and like other members of the family they are fast runners with long legs, but they are not very good fliers. Some species are so accustomed to life on the ground that they have lost the ability to fly, and others have even lost their wings.

Many insects simply take flight when a predator attacks. Bombardier beetles have a very different way of defending themselves. They stand their ground, aim their flexible anus (rear end) at the attacker, and squirt out an explosive blast of boiling-hot toxic chemicals. Sometimes, the blast is accompanied by a popping noise like gunfire and what looks like a puff of smoke. The chemicals are foul-tasting, corrosive, and extremely hot—enough to cause most predators to leap away or spit the beetle out, giving it a chance to run away.

The most common American and European bombardier beetles are less than 0.4 inches (1 cm) long and have a brownish yellow head and legs and dark blue wing covers. They spend the daytime hiding under logs, stones, or leaves, but they come out at night to hunt for caterpillars and insects.

Defensive discharge

The spray produced by bombardiers comes from a pair of glands next to the anus. One contains a mixture of two chemicals: hydroquinone and hydrogen peroxide. Under normal circumstances, these chemicals do not react together.

▼ *The spray of the bombardier is an effective defense against potential predators such as spiders. It is generated by a pair of glands at the rear of the abdomen.*

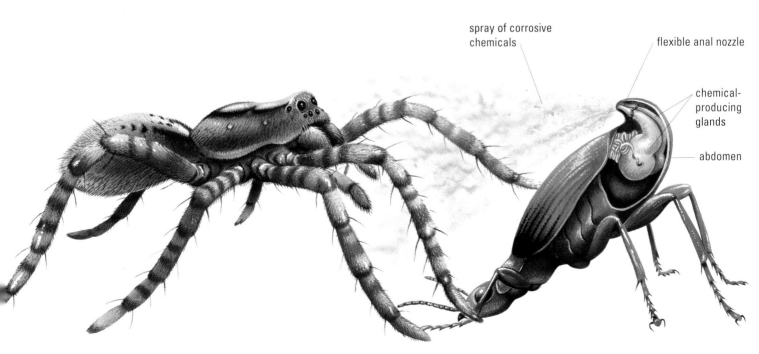

spray of corrosive chemicals

flexible anal nozzle

chemical-producing glands

abdomen

KEY FACTS

Name
Brachinus
bombardier
beetles

Behavior
Adults live in
groups; nocturnal;
use chemical
defense; spend
day under stones

Food
Adults eat insects,
especially caterpil-
lars; larvae feed on
water beetle
pupae

Size
Up to 0.4 inches
(1 cm)

DISTRIBUTION

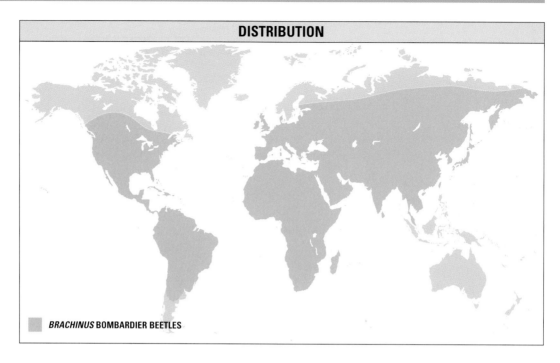

■ *BRACHINUS* BOMBARDIER BEETLES

However, when a bombardier needs to protect itself, the chemicals are squeezed through a one-way valve into the second gland, where an enzyme makes the chemicals react. The reaction releases so much heat and gas that the chemicals explode out at very high temperatures. The tip of the abdomen is highly mobile, allowing the beetle to direct the spray. Nevertheless, some animals have learned how to overcome the bombardier's weapon. Predatory horsefly larvae yank the beetles quickly into mud, birds protect themselves with their feathers, and grasshopper mice are said to jab the beetles tail first into sand.

Strange life cycles

The life cycle of bombardier beetles is just as fascinating as their defensive mechanism. A few days after mating, female *Brachinus pallidus* lay their eggs

▶ *A* Brachinus *bombardier beetle. During the day, these beetles often hide in groups beneath stones.*

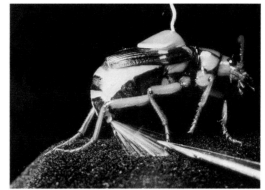

◄ *The bombardier beetle can aim its spray accurately at the source of danger. In these pictures, the defense behavior is caused by gently prodding the beetle with a pair of forceps. The spray is not continuous, but it is squirted out in pulses of about 1,000 squirts per second.*

inside small balls of mud scooped carefully from wet ground near a river or stream. It takes a female about five minutes to make a mud ball and lay a single egg inside it. Then she sticks the mud ball to a rock or twig and leaves it.

The tiny larva that hatches out about a week later looks very different from its parents, with a long, slender body but no wings or wing case. Immediately after hatching, it scuttles off in search of its main source of food: the pupa of a water beetle. Water beetles are also found in wet ground near streams and ponds. When the bombardier larva finds a suitable pupa, it begins to eat its victim head first.

The larva grows quickly, molting several times to let its body expand. After only one or two days, the water beetle pupa has been completely devoured, and all that is left is its hollow case, now containing a fat bombardier larva. This turns into a pupa itself to undergo the process of metamorphosis, where the body liquefies before re-forming as an adult. Finally, the pupa splits open and a new beetle emerges.

Not all bombardier beetle larvae prey on water beetle pupae. Some species feed on the eggs of mole crickets and others on termites. The larvae of one species live in ants' nests, where they trick the ants into bringing them food. Adult bombardiers live in groups that gather under rocks during the day.

Squirting or foaming?

Although most species of bombardier squirt fluids at potential predators, one species does things differently. When attacked from the rear, *Metrius contractus* allows a corrosive foam to build up over the tip of the abdomen. If attacked from the front, it conveys the froth along the body through grooves running over the wing cases. The foam is similar to the liquid discharged by other bombardiers, and it makes the beetle a very unpleasant thing to eat.

Many species of ground beetles discharge defensive chemicals of one sort or another. This ability probably evolved because many of these beetles cannot take to the wing quickly enough to escape a sudden attack.

SEE ALSO

- *Beetle*
- *Defense*
- *Ground beetle*
- *Metamorphosis*
- *Scarab beetle*
- *Tiger beetle*
- *Water beetle*

Booklouse

Booklice have been on Earth for more than 100 million years, a lot longer than books. These tiny insects feed on bark, molds, and bits of dead plants and animals, as well as book glue.

In hot and humid places around the world, tiny insects called booklice often live. Measuring less than 0.2 inches (5 mm) long, they are so small that large numbers can live in a house without being noticed at all. There are 1,100 species found around the world.

Unfortunately, warm but damp human-built structures are perfect for the molds and mildews on which these tiny insects like to feed. Many booklice species live in different parts of people's homes, such as in damp basements, furniture stuffings, and even stored food like cereal or flour, as well as beneath peeling wallpaper and on houseplants. As their name suggests, booklice also feed on the glues and bindings of books and on the fungus that invades the paper. It is because of these habits that they have been given their common name and the nicknames "paper fleas" and "paper lice."

Lice relatives

Booklice are thought to have evolved about 100 million years ago. They share a common ancestor with several other

▼ *Barklice, like the one below, differ from most of their booklouse relatives because they have wings and are commonly found outdoors.*

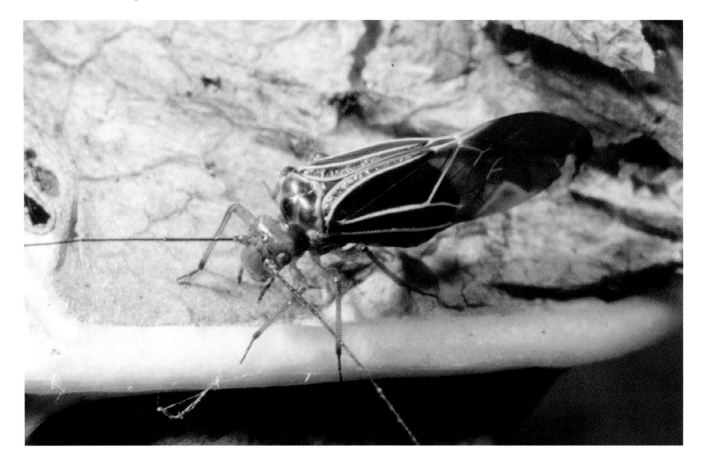

▲ *Many species
of booklice make a
ticking noise by hitting their
abdomen against the ground. Scientists
think lice communicate with these noises.*

groups of insects, including bugs, thrips, and the biting and sucking lice. However, despite the similarities of name, booklice are unlike these other lice because they do not feed on the skin, feathers, or blood of other animals, and they are not closely related to them.

Book and bark

Booklice belong to an order, or group, of insects called the Psocoptera, which also includes similar species called barklice. This scientific name comes from two Latin words: *psoco,* meaning "small rub," and *ptera,* meaning "winged." These insects were given this name because the damage that some species cause when they feed looks like something rough has been wearing away at the surface.

Many species within the group have wings. Winged members are generally those that live on vegetation and under bark, such as barklice. Most booklice

have little need for flight, and over millions of years of evolution their wings have reduced in size, and in many cases have disappeared altogether. Instead of taking to the air, these insects travel around by running very quickly and hopping in a jerky manner along exposed surfaces.

Body form

Booklice have soft, stout bodies that are brown to white and sometimes almost transparent, especially when young. Their fine, threadlike antennae are divided into 12 to 50 segments. The head and abdomen appear large, especially compared to the narrow thorax (midbody).

Booklice mouthparts are specialized for biting and chewing pollen grains, fungi, bacteria, and the decaying tissue of dead animals and plants. Rodlike mouthparts hold the louse above the food, while scraping sections dig away

KEY FACTS

Name
*Liposcelis
corrodens*
booklouse

**Distinctive
Features**
Small size, flesh
colored, with
threadlike
antennae

Distribution
Lives alongside
humans

Breeding
All female, hatch-
ing from unfertil-
ized eggs

Food
Molds, spores,
and book glue

Bark good for a bite

The cousins of booklice, the barklice, are very similar in many ways, except they live outdoors and have wings. When resting, they hold their wings upright above the body almost like the roof of a house.

They are mainly woodland insects and feed mostly on lichens and dead plant matter. In the summer, barklice can be seen as tiny, tan-colored specks on the bark of hardwood and conifer trees, or in the dead leaves and damp wood that lie on the woodland floor. They also live on rocks, fence posts, and even picnic tables and birds' nests.

Because they appear in such very high numbers, barklice are an important part of the food chain in woodland habitats. Spiders prey on these tiny insects, which, in turn, are then eaten by small mammals such as shrews. The shrews are in turn eaten by predators like owls or weasels. Barklice are good dispersers and are often the first insects to colonize new areas, such as those formed by forest fires. Some species of barklice live together in huge groups. Still preferring moist areas, these groups are often found living underneath large silken webs, which they spin on tree trunks.

▼ *A thick web of silk is home to a large group of barklice in Trinidad.*

at the wood, causing the rough, worn away texture associated with these insects. Some species have large eyes that stick out from the sides of the head. However, most have poor vision, as sight is not important for booklice, which often live in dark places.

Booklice rely on sensing the chemicals produced by their food and the vibrations and sounds caused by other lice and predators. Booklice are also unusual since they can spin silk from their mouthparts as both adults and nymphs. They use this material to make protective webs for their eggs.

One reason that booklice prefer damp, humid conditions is that their hard outer covering, or cuticle, is very thin. The cuticle cannot completely prevent these insects from drying out. If the water levels in the air drop below a certain level, booklice become slow moving and inactive. Within just a few hours, they can dry out and die.

Life cycle

Many booklouse populations are entirely female and develop from unfertilized eggs. Species that reproduce in this way are described as asexual.

The females lay smooth pearl-colored oval eggs, often near a food source that the young insects can eat after they

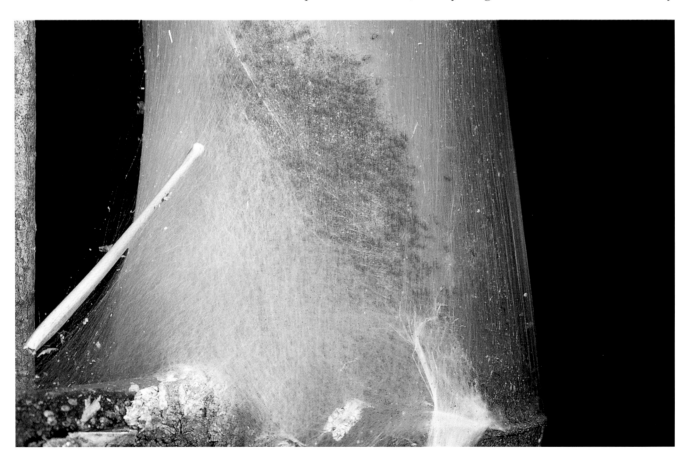

hatch. The sticky eggs are laid either on their own or in clusters at a rate of around one to three eggs per day. After about two weeks or so, the eggs hatch into nymphs. These young forms look like the adults but are extremely tiny and do not move around much.

As the nymphs grow, they molt (shed their skin). Booklice young pass through between four to six nymphal stages, resembling the adult more and more at each stage. This process takes one or two months, or longer if conditions are too cool or dry. An average female booklouse will lay only about 60 eggs in the course of its life.

Adult booklice can sometimes survive for as long as six months, but only if conditions are favorable. Booklice cannot tolerate cold, and if temperatures drop too much during winter, they die. Eggs that are laid close to the onset of winter can survive the cold and hatch out in spring when the weather becomes warmer and moister.

Booklice and people

Since booklice live in houses and other buildings that humans use, they can often be serious pests, especially in a library. In small numbers, they cause very little damage directly when they feed, and most buildings do not get damp enough for a serious infestation.

However, in the right conditions, their numbers can explode and cause infestations that damage delicate materials such as books. A small number of species are agricultural pests that cause severe damage to stores of flour or grain. Although in most cases adult booklice are virtually harmless, their dead and decaying bodies are believed to cause allergic skin reactions and might also trigger attacks of asthma, an illness that causes breathing problems.

▲ *Booklice are tiny insects. People rarely see individual lice, or just mistake them for bits of dust.*

SEE ALSO
- *Biting louse*
- *Bug*
- *Sucking louse*

103

BRUSH-FOOTED BUTTERFLY

With more than 5,000 species, the brush-footed butterflies are the world's largest group of butterflies. These brightly colored insects are a common sight on and around flowers, feeding on nectar.

About a third of the world's butterflies belong to the family known as the brush-footed butterflies. This is the largest butterfly family and includes some of the biggest and most colorful species in the world.

Many brush-foots are well-known, such as the fritillaries, tortoiseshells, painted ladies, and the spectacular blue morpho of South America. Brush-footed butterflies are found worldwide, and there are more than 5,000 species.

These butterflies have tiny front legs, which have bristly ends that look like miniature brushes. These brush feet are totally useless in males, but females use them to check the chemical makeup of plants, helping them find the right place to lay their eggs. Only the four hind legs are used for standing and slowly walking about.

Brightly colored butterflies

Like most butterflies, brush-footed butterflies are active by day, when they fly in search of the nectar (sugary liquid found in flowers) on which they feed. They are powerful fliers, and some, such as the red admiral, migrate for hundreds of miles.

The American painted lady, which is found across North America, sometimes turns up in Europe, having survived the long flight across the Atlantic. It is likely that these butterflies are helped on their journey by strong winds.

The upper surface of the wings is often brilliantly colored or iridescent, while the lower surface is usually camouflaged. To hide from predators, the

butterflies simply land, fold their wings, and keep still. Angelwings, such as the comma butterfly, also have ragged wing margins that make their folded wings look remarkably like dead leaves. This camouflage fools predators.

Coloration

Many brush-footed butterflies protect themselves by mimicking the color or markings of poisonous or inedible butterflies. One such cheat is the American viceroy, which is very hard to tell apart from the monarch butterfly. Birds that try eating the foul-tasting monarch soon learn to leave it alone.

▲ *This mourning cloak is a brush-footed butterfly. Like most members of this group, the bright colors only occur on the wings' upper surfaces.*

DISTRIBUTION

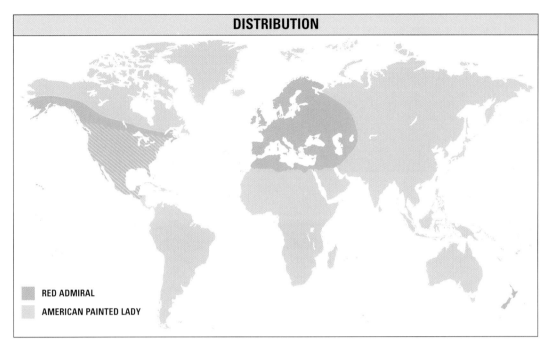

RED ADMIRAL

AMERICAN PAINTED LADY

KEY FACTS

Name
Red admiral
(*Vanessa atalanta*)

Distinctive Features
Bright red and black with white spots; caterpillar, black with white and yellow spots

Habitat
Open woodland, gardens, and meadows

Breeding
Lays single eggs on tips of nettle leaves

Food
Caterpillar eats nettles; adult eats nectar, sap, and rotten fruit

Size
Wingspan: 2.5 inches (63 mm)

However, they will also avoid the viceroy, despite the fact that they are a tasty meal. Peacock butterflies have bright eyespots on their wings that startle birds, giving themselves a few seconds to escape an attack.

Eggs and caterpillars

Most adult brush-footed butterflies lead very short lives of only two to four weeks, although some can survive for months by spending winter in a resting state. Although nectar is rich in energy, it contains few other nutrients, and butterflies therefore depend on the reserves of essential protein and minerals they built up as caterpillars.

In mild climates, brush-footed butterflies are most often seen in spring and summer, when flowers and nectar are most abundant. Females typically lay round, ribbed eggs on leaves, often in large groups.

The caterpillars are often adorned with sharp spines, horns, or other projections to ward off predators, and many have

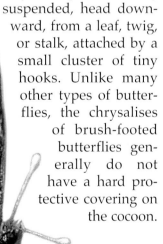

warning colors to advertise that they are poisonous or inedible. In some species, the caterpillars stay together in large groups, providing safety in numbers. After around five moltings, the caterpillars turn into pupae (which in butterflies are called chrysalises) and begin to metamorphose (change) into adults.

The pupae of brush-footed butterflies often have warty bumps and hang suspended, head downward, from a leaf, twig, or stalk, attached by a small cluster of tiny hooks. Unlike many other types of butterflies, the chrysalises of brush-footed butterflies generally do not have a hard protective covering on the cocoon.

◄ *Adult brush-footed butterflies feed mainly on nectar produced by flowers. In turn, they help to transfer pollen from flower to flower.*

SEE ALSO

- *Blue butterfly*
- *Glasswing butterfly*
- *Monarch butterfly*
- *Morpho butterfly*
- *Moth and butterfly*

BUG

People often use the word *bug* to describe almost any kind of insect. To scientists, however, a bug is a member of just one group of insects. All bugs have piercing and sucking mouthparts for feeding on liquids.

Some of the most familiar bugs are not bugs at all. For example, ladybugs and lightningbugs are beetles. Pill bugs and sow bugs are not even insects but crustaceans related to shrimps and lobsters. However, entomologists use the word *bug* to refer to a single group of insects called the Hemiptera.

Hemiptera means "half-winged," referring to the fact that most bugs have forewings that are thick and leathery near the body, and thin and membrane-like at the tips. All members of the Hemiptera have beaklike mouthparts to feed on the fluids of plant and animals.

Different types of bug

Bugs are divided into four subgroups. The first is the true bugs. The distinct beaklike mouthparts of the true bugs extend backward beneath the body and can be extended forward in order to feed. The majority of true bugs feed primarily on plant sap or prey on other insects. Bed bugs are a type of true bug that drink the blood of larger animals, including humans.

Cicadas, hoppers, and spittlebugs form another group. They have short, bristlelike antennae and mouthparts and feet with three segments. They are sap (plant fluid) feeders. Most species are fully winged and strong flyers.

The aphids, whiteflies, and scales form the third subgroup. Their mouthparts join the body between their front pair of legs. The feet of these insects have only one or two segments and their antennae are long and threadlike, or occasionally absent.

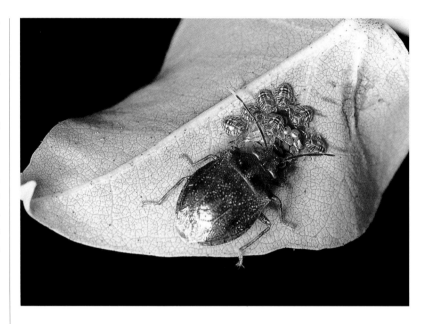

The final group contains only a very few species found in Australia, New Zealand, and South America.

What do bugs feed on?

Nearly all bugs are restricted to a liquid diet. They feed on plant sap, fungi, blood, or solid food that has been liquefied with digestive juices. Cicadas, hoppers, aphids, whiteflies, and scales are strictly sap feeders. Both adults and nymphs of this species tap directly into the tubelike vessels that transport sugary solutions around the plant.

The majority of true bugs, such as leaf-footed bugs, also feed on plant sap. Leaf-footed bugs are so named because the legs of some species are flattened and leaflike or enlarged with spines. Assassin bugs are skilled predators that stalk or ambush their victims. These bugs are capable of killing and consum-

▲ *This shield bug is guarding her newly-hatched nymphs. Although it is rare for insects to look after their young, several types of bugs do it.*

ing insects many times their size. They produce toxic saliva that paralyzes, kills, and then liquefies the internal organs of their prey, which they then suck back up. Ambush bugs are flattened with rough-edged expansions on their bodies that conceal them while they lie in wait for prey.

The saliva of blood-feeding bugs contains anticoagulants—chemicals that prevent the blood from clotting. A few bugs, including the cone-nose bugs and bed bugs, feed on the blood of mammals, including humans.

Underwater bugs

While most bugs live on land, some live on, in, or near ponds or quiet streams. Nearly all of these are predators, attacking insects, crustaceans, and other small animals, and some even feed on

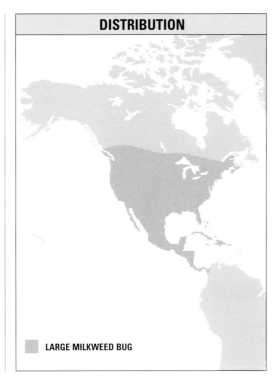

DISTRIBUTION

LARGE MILKWEED BUG

KEY FACTS

Name
Large milkweed bug (*Oncopeltus fasciatus*)

Distinctive features
Bright orange and black

Breeding
Females lay eggs in the cottony fibers of milkweed seed pods

Food
Dried seeds, especially those of milkweed

Size
0.3 to 0.75 inches (8 to 19 mm) long

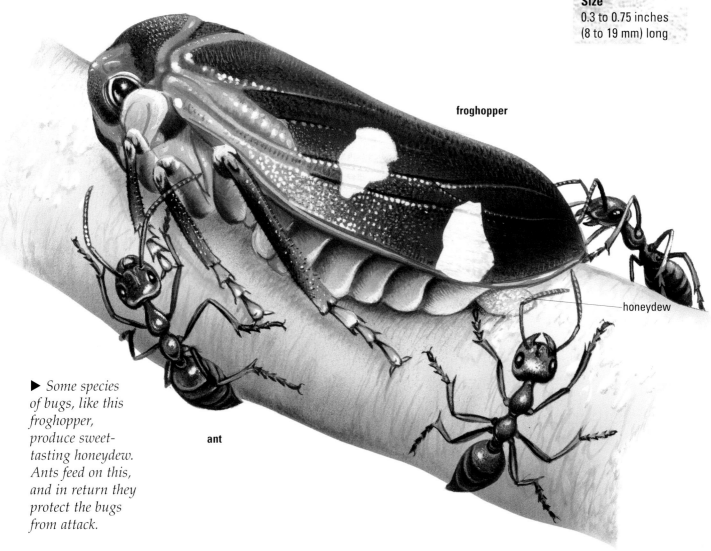

froghopper

honeydew

ant

▶ *Some species of bugs, like this froghopper, produce sweet-tasting honeydew. Ants feed on this, and in return they protect the bugs from attack.*

▶ *Some bugs are fierce predators of other insects. This spined soldier beetle is feeding on a Mexican bean beetle larva, a serious pest of crops such as soybeans. The bug is using its long, pointed mouthparts to suck the juices from its prey. These bugs are used by scientists and farmers in biological control programs.*

tadpoles and small fish. Most aquatic bugs have streamlined bodies and flattened legs adapted for swimming. The oarlike hind legs of water boatmen are used for swimming, while their middle legs help anchor them to underwater objects. The hind legs of backswimmers are flattened and are used like oars to propel them upside down through quiet pools and lakes. The middle and front legs are used to grasp insect prey. Water scorpions are in fact bugs. They do not have legs modified for swimming and generally stay close to the water's surface.

The claws of water striders are placed back from the tip of their feet to prevent them from breaking through the surface film. The middle and hind legs are long and are used to propel the water strider across the water, while the much shorter forelegs are used for capturing food. These bugs feed on insects that fall into the water. The insect's struggles send ripples across the water surface, alerting the water strider to its presence.

Aquatic bugs living under water carry their air with them. Giant water bugs trap an air bubble between their wings by pointing the tip of their abdomen above water. Water boatmen poke their head and thorax through the water surface to capture an air bubble beneath their body. Backswimmers acquire their air supply by breaking the surface film with the tip of their abdomen and drawing an air bubble along their back. Water scorpions, however, breathe air directly through a long, snorkel-like tube attached to the abdomen.

Mouthparts

The mouthparts of a bug are made up of two sections. The outer section is called the rostrum. The tip of the rostrum is used to taste the surface of the food.

When a suitable food supply is located, the rostrum is pulled back, exposing the second, inner section, called the stylet. The sharp stylet is plunged into the food. The stylet is hollow, so digestive juices and liquid food can travel up or down it.

◀ *A large milkweed bug at rest on a twig. The bug's orange coloration warns predators that the insect is foul-tasting. These bugs feed on milkweed, a plant that is filled with poisons.*

KEY FACTS

Name
Leafhopper
(Family
Cicadellidae)

Distinctive features
Small insects with spiny hind legs

Habitat
Plant stems
and leaves

Behavior
Strong jumpers;
adults and nymphs
move sideways
to keep the plant
between them
and attackers

Breeding
Eggs laid on plants

Food
Plant sap

Parental care

Bugs lay their eggs singly or in groups on or in plant tissues. After depositing the eggs, most female bugs wander away, never to see their young again. The eggs are vulnerable to attack by various predators and parasites. In some species, the females (and rarely, the males) remain with the eggs and nymphs to provide protection. Female treehoppers will sit on top of their pile of eggs, responding to any threats with buzzing sounds. Some flap their wings to startle attackers or to fan noxious chemicals in their direction. Some female stinkbugs will defend their eggs by leaning sharply in the direction of a perceived threat. Even after the eggs hatch, the stinkbug will continue to protect her nymphs by kicking and flapping her wings. Some leaf-footed bugs protect their eggs by shooting a stream of smelly fluid at would-be attackers.

Female giant water bugs lay their eggs in clusters on stems

▶ *The pointed mouthparts of a bug are made up of a movable outer rostrum and a piercing, hollow stylet.*

above the water, where the males guard them. The female of another type of giant water bug lays her eggs on the back of the male, and he carries them until they hatch.

Defensive tactics

To protect themselves, many true bugs discourage their enemies by producing strong odors. Stinkbugs and others have glands near the base of their hind legs that emit a strong, sometimes disagreeable odor to repel attackers.

Although most seed bugs are dull in color, the large milkweed bug is bright orange and black and 0.30 to 0.75 inches (8 to 19 mm) long. Its bright, contrasting colors warn

predators of the bug's bad taste, a result of a diet of poisonous milkweed.

The pointed, thornlike midsection of some treehoppers may serve as camouflage for those that feed on thorny plants, and to discourage predators. The nymphs lack this developed midsection and are usually covered with short, sharp spines. Both treehoppers and aphids produce honeydew, a sugary waste product highly attractive to ants. The ants will defend their sources of honeydew by driving off other insects such as ladybugs and parasitic wasps. The nymphs of spittlebugs hide within a foamy mass of bubbles they produce as

◀ *Metallic coloration, seen here on a shield bug, is common within the group. This bug is sucking plant sap from a leaf.*

▼ *These are boxelder bug nymphs. They feed on the sap of many common trees, such as ash and maple.*

ANATOMY OF A SHIELD BUG

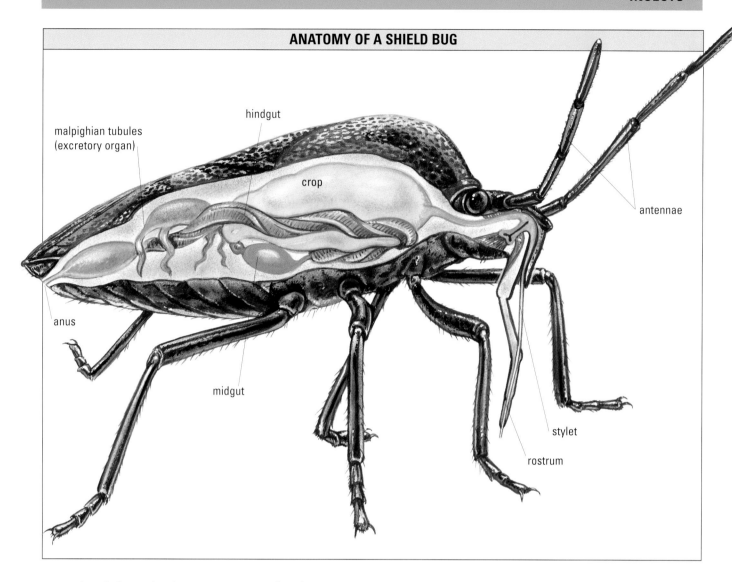

malpighian tubules
(excretory organ)

hindgut

crop

antennae

anus

midgut

stylet

rostrum

a result of their feeding activities. The winged adults are known as froghoppers for their powerful jumping ability.

Bugs and humans

Aphids, leafhoppers, seed bugs, and mealy bugs are all bugs that are important pests to human crops. Their feeding activities weaken greenhouse plants, reduce agricultural yields, and infect plants with diseases. Sooty fungus may grow on the honeydew produced by many of these pests. The fungus stops sunlight from reaching the leaf, which prevents the plant from trapping the light's energy to make food; this leads to severe weakening or even death.

Humans use some aquatic bugs as food. Giant water bugs are the largest bugs in the world, reaching 6 inches

(15 cm) long. In some parts of Asia, these bugs are boiled in brine, dried, and eaten like biscuits. Their scent glands are even ground up into a paste and used as a spicy condiment. In Mexico, the eggs and adults of backswimmers are eaten by humans as well as being sold as pet food.

For centuries, the waxy and resinous secretions of scale insects have provided humans with cosmetics, traditional medicines, and candles. The secretions of the lac insect are the source of shellac, a thin clear varnish, which was also used to make the first gramophone records, while the cochineal insect was an important source of red dye used in cosmetics, foods, and drinks, although it has largely been replaced by less expensive artificial alternatives.

▲ *Plant sap is composed mainly of water. The large intestine of a plant bug is very good at removing this water from its food.*

SEE ALSO

- *Aphid*
- *Assassin bug*
- *Bedbug*
- *Leaf bug*
- *Mealybug*
- *Scale*
- *Sea skater*
- *Stinkbug*
- *Water bug*
- *Whitefly*

BULLDOG ANT

The bulldog ant of Australia is well known for its vicious bite and painful sting, which can cause a dangerous allergic response in some people. Many a picnic has been ruined by these large and aggressive ants, which are unusual in that they have a very different social system from other ants.

Bulldog ants are easy to recognize. They are much larger than most ants, measuring up to about 0.8 inches (2 cm) long, and they have a pair of very large mandibles (jaws) that look like tiny saws. They also have large, bulging eyes and are bright red and black. Their development, behavior, and social systems are very different from those of other species of ants.

Bulldog ants live in colonies founded by a queen. The eggs, larvae, and pupae are tended by worker ants, all of which are female. Workers also defend the nest from attack from predators.

Feeding

The workers are skillful and nimble hunters. During the day, they search the ground and low bushes for spiders and insects, including other ants. They hunt by stealth, using their excellent vision to locate prey, and then wait motionless with mandibles wide apart for the victim to come within striking range. Then, with a sudden dash, they snatch the prey with their mandibles and cripple it with a lethal sting; the stingers are located at the tip of the abdomen. The prey is usually taken back to be fed to the larvae; the workers themselves feed mostly on nectar. When there are only a few larvae in the nest, workers rarely take food back.

Other ants commonly share food with each other. This does not occur in bulldog ants; even the queen must forage for her own food. Bulldog ants'

nests are located underground and contain only a few hundred individuals. Most ants have a complex vocabulary of communication techniques. By contrast, bulldog ants show only a limited range of interactions between individuals. Although they release alarm chemicals called pheromones in times of danger, they do not lay down scent trails showing the way to feeding sites.

Most of the young develop into wingless workers, but a few grow into new queens or into males, both of which have wings. In several species of bulldog ants, these winged forms fly away from the nest and gather in swarms to mate. Sometimes, the queens are so outnumbered by the males that each queen might be covered by a ball of struggling ants as big as a persons fist. Other species have different mating

▲ *Bulldog ants have very large mandibles, which can give a painful nip. Large eyes give them excellent vision, which is essential for capturing prey.*

strategies. In one species, the queens lose their wings while still in the nest, then wander around on the ground, while the males fly to locate them.

Most new queens fall victim to predators soon after leaving the nest, but a few manage to breed and find a suitable site for a new colony, sometimes in partnership with another queen. They store the sperm collected during mating in a reservoir at the rear of the abdomen, and they use it to fertilize eggs throughout their lives. The workers can lay eggs as well—these either hatch as males or are used as food.

A painful bite

Attacks on humans occur when people accidentally stray into the territory of a colony. Some of the workers act as sentinels, standing guard above ground within a few feet of the nest. If a person disturbs one of these sentinels, it runs around wildly in search of its nestmates, which then do the same, once the first ant has made contact. Soon, the alarm spreads to the nest, and reinforcements emerge to drive off the intruder. The large mandibles can deliver a powerful

DISTRIBUTION

BULLDOG ANTS

bite, but the sting is much more painful. Like many ants, bulldog ants produce a venom containing a toxic substance called formic acid, and they combine this with another substance, called histamine, as well as other proteins. This cocktail is lethal to invertebrates, while in humans and other large animals it causes acute pain and a red swelling in the skin. It can sometimes produce a severe allergic reaction needing urgent attention.

Bulldog ants live throughout Australia and on some of the surrounding islands. There are 89 known species, one of which also lives in New Caledonia, and another has been found living in Auckland, New Zealand. This species was probably introduced to the area from Australia by people.

KEY FACTS

Name
Bulldog ants
(*Myrmecia*
species)

Distinctive Features
Large red and black body; bulbous eyes; large sawlike mandibles

Behavior
Lives in underground nests with few hundred individuals; very aggressive

Breeding
Fertilized eggs hatch into females; unfertilized eggs hatch into males

Food
Larva: insects and spiders; adult: nectar

Size
Up to 0.8 inches (20 mm) long

SEE ALSO
- *Ant*
- *Army ant*
- *Fire ant*
- *Honeypot ant*
- *Slave-maker ant*
- *Weaver ant*
- *Wood ant*

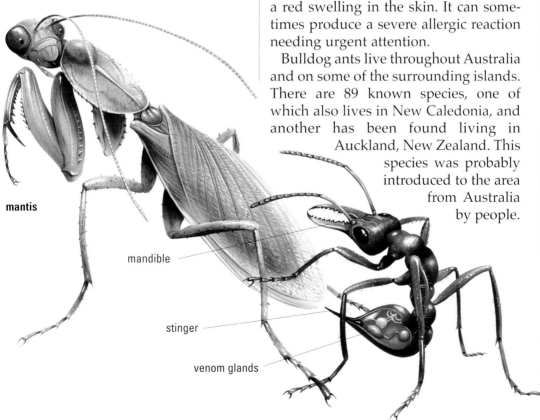

mantis

mandible

stinger

venom glands

◀ *Bulldog ants both bite and sting their insect prey, such as this large mantis, as well as human intruders.*

BUMBLEBEE

With a queen bee in charge of the colony, bumblebees work together to raise the next generation. By feeding on pollen and nectar, these insects also help many plants to reproduce.

Bumblebees belong to a family of hairy insects called the Apidae, which contains around 1,000 species, including, among many others, the honeybee. All bees are part of the order Hymenoptera, along with wasps, ants, and sawflies. Like all Hymenoptera, bumblebees have two pairs of wings that are joined by small hooks along the front edge of the hind wing.

The bumblebee body

Bumblebees range from 0.1 to 1.2 inches (2.5 mm to 30 mm) long, and are covered with a layer of stiff hairs that help the bee to keep warm. Adult bees are generally black, with varying numbers of yellow, red, or orange bands. The common name of the bee describes its coloration, as in the buff-tailed bumblebee.

A stinger in the tail

Like honeybees, bumblebees have a stinger they can use to defend themselves and their nests. However, unlike honeybees, bumblebees do not leave the stinger in their victims and can live to strike again. (Honeybees die after leaving their stinger in the victim.) A bee's stinger is a modified ovipositor (egg tube); in other insects, it is used for laying eggs. Most female bumblebees are workers and cannot reproduce, so their ovipositor is used as a stinger. Bumblebees are generally placid creatures, but if threatened they can use their stinger to repel or injure attackers.

Warning colors

The combination of a tough hairy body, a stinger, and a repellent taste makes a bumblebee a particularly unpleasant prey item. Experienced predators learn to leave bee-colored animals alone after a few unpleasant encounters. People also learn to avoid yellow and black insects for fear of receiving a painful sting. This is good news for bumble-

◀ A bumblebee's long proboscis helps the insect reach the sugary nectar deep inside a flower. As it feeds, the bee also collects pollen on its legs.

DISTRIBUTION

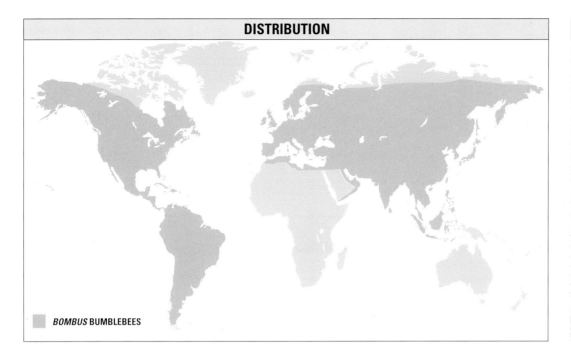

BOMBUS BUMBLEBEES

KEY FACTS

Name
Bombus
bumblebees

Distinctive Features
Hairy bodies, two pairs of wings, yellow, orange, or red stripes

Breeding
Single female queen produces nonbreeding workers; males develop from unfertilized eggs

bees, and also for the many other insect species that look similar to them, such as hover flies and bee flies. When one species imitates another in this way it is called mimicry. Despite their apparent distastefulness, bumblebees are still eaten by some animals, including skunks, mice, and birds.

A social animal

Bumblebees live together in colonies, as do termites, honeybees, ants, and some species of wasps. Just like honeybees, there is a single reproductive female, called a queen, in each bumblebee nest, and she lays all the eggs. However, unlike honeybees, only the queen

▼ *A female cuckoo bumblebee can be seen (left) stealing pollen from a bumblebee colony, while the queen (right) is totally unaware.*

bumblebee survives winter, and the rest of the colony die off during frosts. In spring, the queens emerge from their sheltered overwintering spot (often underground) to feed and search for a new nest. The nest may be underground in an abandoned mousehole or above-ground among grass or moss. The queen makes the nest warm and dry using natural fibers such as grass, moss, or animal hair.

When conditions are suitable, the queen uses wax-producing glands on her body to produce a small cell. She then gathers pollen and places it in the cell, eventually laying her eggs among the pollen. When the larvae emerge, they are pale and grublike, lack legs, and have no obvious head. They feed on the pollen that the queen has stored in the cell. The queen may also store nectar in wax pots within the nest for the growing larvae to feed on.

When the larvae have completed their development, they spin silken cocoons and turn into pupae. Despite having legs and a head during this stage, the bee pupae remain inactive.

The queen's young are produced from eggs fertilized the previous year, and initially they are tended by her alone. Fertilized eggs yield female young, but these are very different from the queen since they cannot reproduce. The duties of these sterile females, called workers, are to tend to the queen and the nest and to feed and look after the queen's new offspring. Once there are enough workers, the queen takes no further part in rearing the young that she continues to produce. Compared to those of many social insects, bumblebee nests are small and rarely have more than a few hundred individuals.

Later in the year, the queen produces some different offspring—the drones, or male bees, which develop from unfertilized eggs. She also produces several female offspring that grow into new queens. When the drones and queens have completed their development,

▼ *An illustration of a cuckoo bee stinging a bumblebee queen to death to steal food for her own larvae.*

they fly off to find mates from other nests. Having mated, the males die, but mated queens seek out a sheltered place where they sit out the winter before starting their own colony in the spring.

Cuckoo bees and other threats
Bumblebee colonies face many dangers, especially from cuckoo bumblebees. These species break into the nests of other bumblebees. When inside, the female cuckoo bee lays her eggs inside the egg chambers and may even kill the

Keeping the chill out
Insects are cold-blooded; that is, generally they cannot generate their own body heat. On cold days, an insect's body processes are slower than on hot days. When cold, insects are sluggish and may not be able to fly. Bumblebees can fly at lower temperatures than most insects because they have a thick coat of hairs, and they can also rapidly tense and relax their flight muscles in a sort of shiver to help them warm up.

bumblebee queen. The cuckoo bee's larvae then eat the food the worker bees continue to provide as they did for their own colony. Some cuckoo bees even eat young bumblebees.

Bees, flowers, and pollen
While cuckoo bees look similar to bumblebees, they can be distinguished by their lack of a pollen-collecting basket on their hind legs. Bumblebees use these baskets to store and transport pollen from flowers to the nest. Bumblebees also have long tubelike mouthparts called a proboscis, which they use to suck up nectar from flowers. Pollen and nectar are both food for bumblebees.

When adult bumblebees visit flowers to collect this food, they also move pollen from flower to flower. In doing this, they fertilize the flowers, allowing them to produce seeds. Bumblebees are responsible for a great deal of the flowering plant pollination that occurs throughout the world.

▲ *A bumblebee approaches a bluebell. Bluebells bloom in early spring, and bumblebees are one of only a few insects that can fly during this cool time of year.*

SEE ALSO
- *Africanized bee*
- *Bee*
- *Bee fly*
- *Communication*
- *Honeybee*
- *Pollination*
- *Social insect*

CADDIS FLY

Imagine a snail that could not grow its own shell but instead had to make one out of sand grains or pieces of plant. Something very similar can be seen in the group of insects called caddis flies, which have larvae that are remarkable for the carefully constructed cases they make to protect themselves.

Caddis flies are common insects that live in freshwater habitats all over the world. Around 10,000 species are known, including more than 1,300 in North America. The adults are mothlike in appearance, while the larvae (young forms) live under water. The caddis flies' nearest relatives are the moths and butterflies. Even so, these two groups appear to have evolved separately for at least 200 million years.

Ecology and distribution

Caddis flies form a major part of the freshwater food chain, being eaten by many fish and some birds. In cool climates, their life cycle commonly lasts a year, and it is the larvae that must survive through the winter.

Caddis flies are believed to have first appeared in cool, fast-flowing streams, where the greatest variety of species is now found. Caddis flies prefer clear unpolluted waters, and the presence or absence of particular species is widely used as an indicator of the degree of pollution within a stream or lake.

One unusual group of caddis flies, found in New Zealand, are among the very few truly marine (sea-living) insects. Females lay their eggs in the bodies of starfish. When they hatch, the larvae live in shallow water nearby.

Caddis fly larvae

Most caddis fly larvae protect and disguise themselves by making tube-shaped cases, which they drag with

DISTRIBUTION

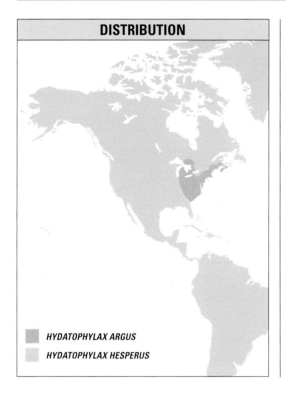

■ HYDATOPHYLAX ARGUS
■ HYDATOPHYLAX HESPERUS

◀ *An adult caddis fly flies toward a cuckoo flower during the night to feed on nectar.*

KEY FACTS

Name
Caddis fly
(Order Trichoptera)

Distinctive Features
Adults are mothlike, with hairs on wings

Behavior
Larvae live under water; most species build protective cases from wood, vegetation, and shells or use silk nets to catch food

Lifespan
About one year

them as they crawl around. Some species construct cases of sand grains, while others make use of plant stalks, wood, or leaf fragments. These are bound together with sticky silk produced by glands near the mouth. The cases are not completely safe, however, because fish often eat larva and case in one gulp.

Caddis fly larvae mainly eat dead material such as leaves, or tiny plantlike algae, although some are carnivores. They enlarge their cases as they grow, as well as molting their skin several times. The larvae themselves have three pairs of legs, plus two hooks at their rear end to grip their cases.

At the back of the case there is generally a small hole, allowing the larva to maintain a water current through the tube. This allows oxygen-rich water to

▼ *The larvae of some types of caddis fly make underwater fishing nets from silk. Scraps of food are filtered from the water by the net.*

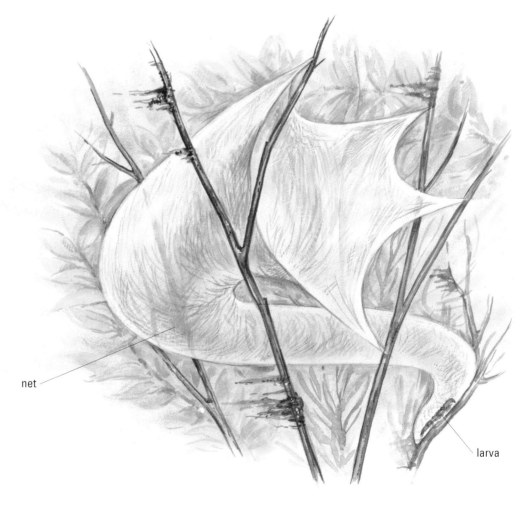

net

larva

CADDIS FLY CASES

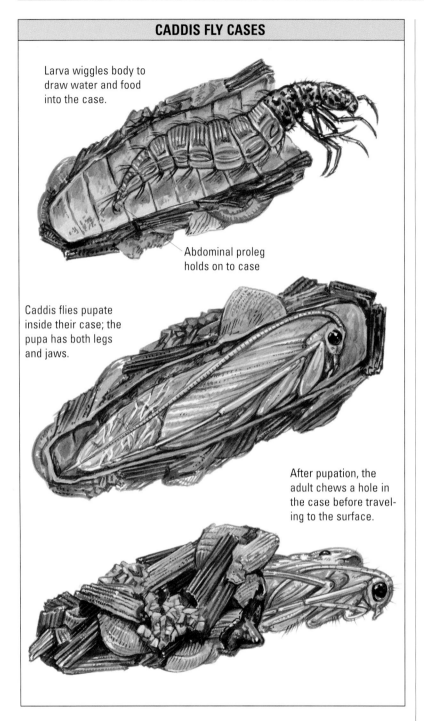

Larva wiggles body to draw water and food into the case.

Abdominal proleg holds on to case

Caddis flies pupate inside their case; the pupa has both legs and jaws.

After pupation, the adult chews a hole in the case before traveling to the surface.

▲ *Caddis fly larvae make a protective case from objects they find under water. They stay in the case during pupation and only emerge as adults.*

freely pass the gills, which run down both sides of the body. The gills act like the larva's lungs, extracting oxygen from the water so the larva can breathe.

Some types of caddis fly do not build cases. Instead, the larvae construct nets out of silk, anchoring these at the bottom of a stream or pond. Different species make nets of different designs; some are like miniature fishing nets, while others form branched tubes through which the larva draws a current. The nets trap small food particles, which the larvae eat. Some species also construct a shelter for themselves nearby. One caddis fly group does not build cases or nets; the larvae are carnivorous and roam freely in search of prey.

Pupae

When a larva is fully grown, it molts to become a nonfeeding stage, or pupa, in which the tissues of the adult are formed from those of the larva. Unlike the pupae of butterflies and moths, the caddis fly pupa is active, having legs and jaws. Case-building larvae anchor their cases to stones and block up their entrances before pupating.

When development is complete, the pupa bites through its protective case to release itself. Then, depending on the species, it either crawls to the water's edge or rises up to the surface, sometimes with the help of air bubbles it has accumulated in its body. Once at the surface, the adult emerges from the pupal skin, expands and dries its wings, then flies off.

Adults

At first glance, adult caddis flies look a bit like moths. Moths, however, have wings covered with scales, while caddis fly wings have small hairs instead. Scientists call the caddis fly group Trichoptera, meaning "hair wings." The wings are generally dull brown or gray, and the hairs give them a patterned appearance. Adult flies hold their wings in a triangle, like a roof, over the body when they are at rest.

Caddis fly antennae are long and thin, sometimes much longer than the body. The adult's jaws cannot be used for feeding, but nectar is sometimes sipped. A few small spines on the legs, called spurs, which vary in number between families, are used to classify these insects into related groups.

Adults may emerge from their pupae at any time from spring to late fall depending on the species. They fly

◀ This caddis fly larvae is a predator. It does not have a case but lives under water feeding on animals such as other insect larvae.

▼ This mass of shell fragments is a caddis fly larva's case. Some of the case is made up of living snails.

mainly at night or in twilight and live for a few weeks or months. Some species come together in swarms that hover over or near water. Individuals join these swarms to find mates. Caddis flies also secrete smelly chemicals called pheromones to attract a mate. To mate, the male and female caddis fly usually settle on the ground or cling to a piece of vegetation.

After mating, the females lay batches of up to several hundred eggs, either under water, on overhanging branches, or on stones beside streams. The egg batches include a substance that swells on contact with water and glues the eggs to stones or plants.

Fly fishing

Experienced fishers are often experts on the appearance and habits of caddis flies. They make or buy artificial flies that look like all stages of the caddis fly's life and use them as bait to tempt fish—especially trout—to take a bite. Larvae, pupae, live adults, and dead

floating adults are all imitated by fishers, although the imitations must be used in the right habitat, and at the right time of day or year, to trick fish. There are even fishers' flies made to look like an adult that has got stuck halfway as it emerges from its pupal skin.

SEE ALSO

- Alderfly
- Defense
- Dragonfly and damselfly
- Mayfly

121

CARPENTER ANT

Most species of carpenter ants excavate their nests in decaying wood and trees. However, a few sometimes burrow into the timber in our homes, causing a great deal of damage.

The name carpenter ant is well deserved. These large ants use their mandibles (jaws) to chew their way into both rotting and solid wood, producing tiny tunnels and chambers with walls so smooth that they appear to be sandpapered. The ants do not eat the wood, as termites do, but discard it in tiny heaps of sawdust. Large colonies can contain up to 10,000 ants, and together these can severely weaken important structural timbers in a house. Carpenter ants are large—up to half an inch (13 mm) long—and range from reddish yellow to jet black. They are most active at night, when the workers leave the nest in great numbers to forage for food.

Feeding

Carpenter ants have a varied diet, including insects, dead animals, nectar, fruit, and honeydew (the sugary liquid produced by aphids). In people's homes, the ants will also eat fruit, meat, and fat, such as butter. On the way back to the nest, the ants leave a scent trail by secreting marker chemicals, or pheromones, from their hindgut. This

▼ *Black carpenter workers care for the ant larvae inside the nest.*

DISTRIBUTION

BLACK CARPENTER ANT

colony grows quickly. After several years, there may be many thousands of workers, divided into two types. Smaller workers look after the eggs and larvae. Larger ants forage for food and also guard the colony against intruders such as other ants.

Tunneling through wood

Although serious pests, carpenter ants play an important ecological role in their natural forest habitat by helping to recycle wood. They usually begin their nests in decaying wood, which is soft and easy to excavate. Once the ants have gained access to a tree through a decayed area, they may extend the nest into healthier timber, following the wood grain and tunneling into softer wood first. They prefer hardwoods, but they can also be found nesting in a

KEY FACTS

Name
Black carpenter ant (*Camponotus pennsylvanicus*)

Behavior
Burrows in wood

Breeding
Mating ants swarm in spring

Food
Insects, fruit, carrion, domestic foodstuffs

Size
0.3 to 0.5 inches (8 to 13 mm)

trail helps other ants find the food source. Large items of food are carried back to the nest in the mandibles. Solid food is fed to the larvae, which regurgitate it in a more easily digestible, liquid form. This is then shared with other workers and with the queen ant.

Founding a new colony

Most of the ants in a colony are female workers that develop from fertilized eggs laid by the queen. The workers are wingless and unable to reproduce, spending their whole lives serving the needs of the colony. The queen also lays eggs that develop into males and females that are both fertile and have wings; these are called alates. The alates fly away from their colonies in spring or early summer to swarm together and mate. The males die soon after mating, but the females look for suitable sites to start new colonies. These new queens lay a small clutch of eggs that hatch and eventually develop into workers. When the workers emerge from their cocoons, they immediately start collecting food and extending the nest into the wood. There are only between 10 and 20 workers during the first year, but the

variety of other tree species. The main nest is usually located in the base of a tree trunk, with galleries extending into the roots and several feet up into the tree. The ants enter the nest through a network of underground tunnels, which may extend for a considerable distance away from the tree.

There are 1,000 different species of carpenter ants in the world. One of the most destructive is the black carpenter ant, which lives throughout the eastern United States and southern Canada.

▲ *Only a few species of carpenter ants are pests in our homes. Most nest inside trees.*

SEE ALSO

- *Ant*
- *Harvester ant*
- *Odorous ant*
- *Pharaoh ant*
- *Termite*

CARPET BEETLE

These beetles eat dried animal remains and can often be found inside animal nests. Some species live in people's homes, where they eat stored food and feed on carpets and furs.

Carpet or larder beetles are small, 0.05 to 0.5 inches (1 to 12 mm) long. They are oval shaped and are generally brown or black. Many species are covered with hairs or small scales. Sometimes, the scales are of different colors, giving the beetles a distinct pattern of black and white bands or colored markings. The heads of carpet beetles are generally not visible from above, being pointed down and tucked under the body. The antennae are clubbed (swollen at the tip) and rest in grooves when folded under the head. The larvae are easily recognized by their hairy or shaggy appearance. There are

▼ *After hatching, larval carpet beetles can cause great damage. After pupation, the adults move to new areas before laying.*

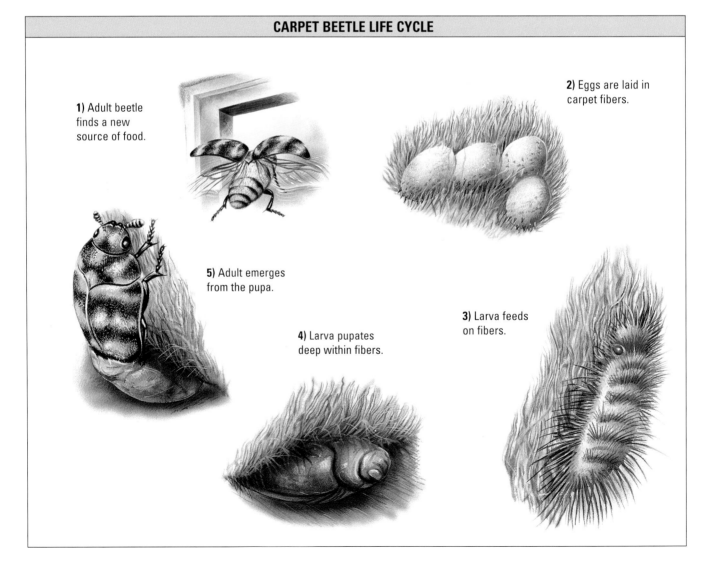

CARPET BEETLE LIFE CYCLE

1) Adult beetle finds a new source of food.

2) Eggs are laid in carpet fibers.

5) Adult emerges from the pupa.

4) Larva pupates deep within fibers.

3) Larva feeds on fibers.

DISTRIBUTION

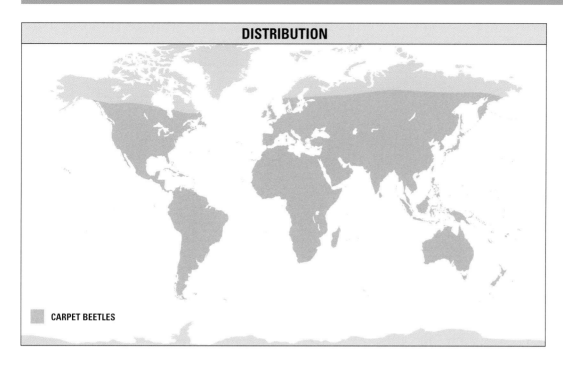

CARPET BEETLES

KEY FACTS

Name
Larder beetle
(*Dermestes
lardarius*)

**Distinctive
features**
Small, black beetle
with white under-
side and broad
band of white
scales across
wing covers

Habitat
Common in houses
and other
buildings; also on
spiderwebs,
dead animals,
nests of birds
and mammals

Breeding
Adult lays 30 to 100
eggs on food;
larval stages last
around 40 days;
pupal stage lasts
around 21 days

Food
Dry animal
material, such as
flesh, skin, fur,
feathers, wool,
and insects

Size
0.2 to 0.4 inches
(5 to 10 mm) long

around 850 species distributed world-wide, with about 130 species found throughout North America.

What do these beetles eat?

These beetles are nearly all scavengers. Adults of a few species are found on flowers, where they eat pollen, but generally they feed on dried animal materials such as insect remains, dry carcasses, hair, skin, fur, or feathers. A few species live in the nests of birds, mammals, or social insects.

Because they are scavengers, a number of carpet beetles are closely associated with humans and their buildings, clothing, and food. They are fond of any items made of natural fibers (such as wool in blankets and carpets) and stored foods, especially those rich in protein, such as meats and cheese. These habits have led to their common names of carpet and larder beetles. Some species are associated with ants, and one species is known to feed on the egg cases of the praying mantis.

◀ *A larder beetle
feeding on cheese.
These beetles can be
important pests to
many foodstuffs.*

125

▲ *Adult carpet beetles feed on organic fibers, but it is their larvae that cause most damage.*

SEE ALSO

- *Beetle*
- *Carrion beetle*
- *Pest*

▶ *An illustration of hide beetles cleaning the dead skin and muscle from animal bones.*

Many carpet beetles have a taste for dried insects. They are commonly found scavenging on the webs of spiders, feeding on the discarded husks of the spider's victims.

Serious pests

Most houses in America have a colony of carpet beetles. When conditions are right, they can multiply quickly to become an important pest. The adults are rarely seen, and it is usually the active, hairy, larval stage that does most of the destructive feeding. Even so, the larvae are often very hard to find and sometimes the only evidence of their presence is their larval skins, which they shed as they grow, or the piles of powdery dust, called frass, which are left behind as they feed.

Carpet beetles are very difficult to control or eliminate. However, only a few species are serious household or economic pests. The khapra beetle feeds on stored grains and agricultural products, and in some parts of the world, it may be the most serious pest of stored foodstuffs.

Friend or foe of the curator

Some beetles are pests in museum collections, where the larvae eat dried skin, fur, feathers, and even insect specimens. Their presence is always of great concern to museum curators. However, the efficient scavenging behavior of these beetles has led to some species, notably the hide beetle, being used to clean the dry flesh and skin from the bones of museum specimens. Many museums keep colonies of these beetles specifically for this purpose. These colonies are often isolated in sealed rooms because of the putrid smell produced as the specimen decomposes.

Before these beetles moved into people's homes, they probably lived in the nests of birds, mammals, bees, and wasps, as some species still do today. Species that sometimes feed on insect collections in museums are also found on spiderwebs.

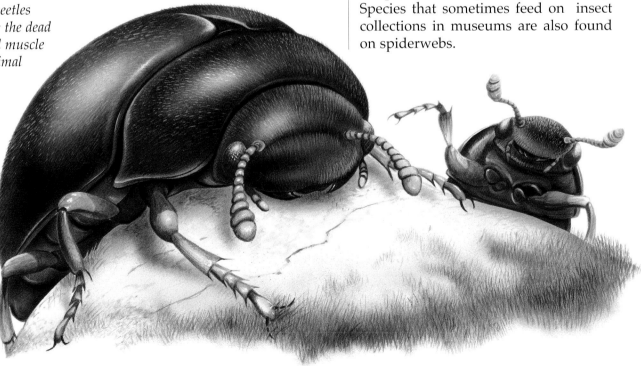

GLOSSARY

abdomen: the rear body section of insects spiders, and other arthropods

alate: a winged adult insect of a species, such as an aphid, that also has adults without wings

antennae (an-TEH-nee): sensitive jointed feelers on the heads of insects

anticoagulant (AN-TY-coh-AHG-yuh-luhnt): chemical released by bloodsucking insects to stop blood from clotting

arthropod (AHR-thruh-PAHD): animal with several pairs of jointed limbs and a hard outer covering (exoskeleton)

carrion: the rotting flesh of dead animals

caterpillar: larva of a butterfly or moth

chrysalis (KRIH-suh-luhs): pupa of a butterfly

convergent evolution: when two unrelated organisms with similar lifestyles look or behave in similar ways

frass: the smelly waste left behind by insects such as cockroaches and carpet beetles

gill: breathing organ of water-living invertebrates and some land-living species, such as pill bugs; it draws in oxygen

halteres (HOL-TIRS): a pair of clublike organs used by flies to balance in flight

honeydew: sugary liquid released by many bugs and some caterpillars as a waste product after feeding on plant sap

host: animal that provides food and usually a place to live for a parasite

insecticide (in-SEHK-tuh-SEYED): a chemical that kills insects

introduction: the release, accidental or otherwise, of animals or plants into a new area

invertebrate (IN-VUHR-tuh-bruht): animal without a backbone

larva (LAR-vuh): young form of insect that looks different from the adult, lives in a different habitat (type of place), and eats different foods

maggot: larva of a fly

metamorphosis (MEH-tuh-MOR-fuh-suhs): change from young form to adult form

mimicry (MIH-mih-kree): when an animal uses color, sound, or behavior to disguise itself as another type of animal, a plant, or even a nonliving object

molt: shedding of the exoskeleton by an arthropod as it grows

nymph (NIMF): young form of insect that looks very similar to the adult and usually lives in a similar habitat (type of place)

ovipositor (OH-vuh-PAH-zuh-tuhr): tube on a female insect's abdomen for laying eggs

oxygen: gas in the air or dissolved in water that all animals need to live

parasite: organism that feeds on another organism called a host; the host may be damaged but is not killed by the parasite

pedipalps (PEH-duh-PALPS): pair of appendages near the mouthparts of spiders that are used for tasting and feeling; male spiders also use them to transfer sperm to females

pheromone (FEH-ruh-MOHN): chemical released by an insect, often to attract mates or to direct other insects to food

phoresy (fuh-REE-see): when a small animal hitches a ride on the body of a larger animal

pollination: transfer of pollen (male sex cells) from one flower to another, either by the wind or by animals such as insects, allowing seeds to form

predator: an animal that feeds by catching and killing other animals

proleg: false leg on the abdomen of some young insects such as caterpillars and caddis fly larvae

pupa (PYOO-puh): stage during which a larva transforms into an adult insect

puparium (pyoo-PAH-ree-uhm): cocoon in which a maggot changes into an adult fly

queen: egg-laying reproductive female in a colony of social insects, including bees, ants, wasps, and termites

sperm: male sex cell that fuses with a female egg to create a new individual

spinneret (SPIH-nuh-REHT): silk-spinning organ at the rear of a spider's abdomen

thorax: midbody section of an insect

vertebrate (VUHR-tuh-bruht): animal with a backbone, such as a bird, reptile, or mammal

INDEX

Page numbers in **bold** refer to main articles; those in *italics* refer to picture captions.

Alates 123
angelwing 104
ant 71, 95, *107*, 110
  bulldog **112–113**
  carpenter **122–123**
aphid 106
arista 90

Backswimmer 108, 111
barklouse *100*, 101, 102
bee 88–89
  bumblebee **114–117**
beetle **68–73**, *76*, 77, 99,
  126
  blister (oil beetle) *72*,
    88–89
  bombardier 72, **97–99**
  carpet (larder beetle)
    124–126
biological control **74–77**
blackfly **81–83**
black widow **85–87**
bloodsucking *82–83*,
  107
blowfly and bluebottle
  90–93
bluebottle *92*, 93
blue butterfly **94–95**
bollworm, cotton 77
booklouse **100–103**
brown widow 85
bug **106–111**
butterfly
  blue **94–95**
  brush-footed **104–105**

Caddis fly **118–121**
camouflage 104
canthidarian 89
caterpillars 95, 105
cicada 106
cochineal 111
courtship, rove
  beetles *71*

Dead, playing 72
defense 72, 109–111
  chemical 72, *97–98*,
    99, *108*
  see also mimicry;
    warning coloration
dye, from insects 111

Earworm, corn *75*
elytra 68
eyespots *95*, 105

Firefly 69, 71
fisher's flies 121
food chains 102, 118
food stealing *115*, *116*
forensic entomology 93
froghopper *107*, 111

Halteres 90
honeydew *107*, 110, 111
hopper 106

Introduced species 74,
  76–77

June bug 71

Ladybug 71, 73, *77*
larvae
  beetle 68–69, 70, 71, 72
  blackfly *83*
  blowfly *90–91*
  caddis fly 118–120,
    121
  see also caterpillars
leafhopper 109
louse, biting **78–80**
  nymphs 79

Mating *71*, *86*
metamorphosis 99
mimicry 72, *89*, *95*,
  104–105, 115

moth, water hyacinth
  75
mourning cloak *104*
mouthparts, bug 108,
  109
museums, and hide
  beetles 126

Nectar *114*, 116

Ovipositor 114

Painted lady 104, *105*
parasites
  biting louse **78–80**
  blackfly **81–83**
parental care, bug 109
pedipalps 86
pest control 72–73, 93
  biological **74–77**
pests
  beetle *70*, 71, 72–73,
    88, *125*, 126
  booklouse 103
  bug 111
  carpenter ant 122
pheromones 69,
  122–123
  mimicry 96
phoresy 89
plants
  controlled with
    insects 76–77
  eaten by beetles
    70–71
poisons 86, 87, 113
pollen, eaten by
  beetles 71
pollen baskets 117
pollination 71, 117
proboscis, bumblebee
  114, 117
pupae *81*, 105, *120*
puparium 91

Red admiral 104, *105*
red widow 85
river blindness *82*, 83
rostrum 108

Sap-feeders 106, *110*,
  111
scale 106, 111
scent trails, ant 122–123
screwworm, New
  World 91, **92–93**
shellac 111
silk 87, *119*
smell, sense of 90
social insects 115–117
spider
  black widow **84–87**
  bolas **96**
spittlebug 106, 110–111
stinkbug *108*, 109

Treehopper 109, 110
triungulin larvae 88, 89

Viceroy, American
  104–105

Warning coloration 72,
  109–110, 114–115
wasp, parasitic *75–76*
water boatman 108
water bug, giant 108,
  109, 111
water life
  bugs 107–108
  caddis flies 118–121
water scorpion 108
water strider 108
webs *84*, 87, *102*
weevil *68*, 69, 70, 71,
  72, 75
whitefly *75*, 106
wireworms 71
wood 70, 122, 123